The Tyranny of the Market

The Tyranny of the Market

WHY YOU CAN'T ALWAYS GET WHAT YOU WANT

Joel Waldfogel

Harvard University Press

Cambridge, Massachusetts

London, England

2007

Library of Congress Cataloging-in-Publication Data

Waldfogel, Joel, 1962–
The tyranny of the market : Why you can't always get what
you want / Joel Waldfogel.
p.   cm.
Includes bibliographical references and index.
ISBN-13: 978-0-674-02581-3
ISBN-10: 0-674-02581-4
1. Consumers' preferences.   2. Majorities.   3. Supply and
demand.   4. Social choice.   5. Free enterprise.   I. Title.
HF5415.32.W35 2007
381—dc22   2007000531

Contents

PART FOUR
POLICY SOLUTIONS AND THEIR LIMITS

Preface

In this book, I respond to—and extend in new ways—ideas laid out most famously in two very important works in economics and political economy, Milton Friedman's *Capitalism and Freedom* and John Stuart Mill's *On Liberty*. Mill points out a fundamental feature of decision-making through government, that majority rule imposes constraints on individuals who disagree with the collective choice. My liberty is abridged in the sense that the choices available to me as a citizen depend on the preferences of others. If the majority wants liquor stores closed on Sunday while I would prefer to have them open, then my freedom is abridged by the fact that we make this choice collectively. If I want green shirts but the state shirt-making collective, bowing to majority views, makes only red, then my freedom to choose among shirt colors is abridged.

Friedman agrees that allocation through collective choice promotes a tyranny of the majority, and he argues that when allocation takes place through markets, rather than collective choice, individuals get what they want rather than, say, what the majority wants. Friedman argues for a stark dichotomy between market and collective choice. Markets offer "freedom" in the sense of allowing people access to whatever products might suit their tastes, regardless of what others prefer. On this basis he argues that societies should let the market decide as many questions as possible to avoid effects akin to tyranny of the majority.

As a student I read both *Capitalism and Freedom* and *On Liberty* with great interest. *Capitalism and Freedom* inspired me with the message that allocation through markets is not just expedient; it also promotes freedom, something far nobler than base material needs. I often claimed to incredulous acquaintances that *Capitalism and Freedom* would still be read centuries from now.

I still view Friedman's book as an enduring contribution, but for more than a decade I have been an empirical economist studying the functioning of actual markets. In the course of my research I have discovered a (growing) number of contexts in which people's consumption options—and indeed their ensuing satisfaction as consumers—depend on the preferences of others. In particular, in markets where fixed costs are substantial and preferences differ across groups of consumers, individuals find more options—and more satisfaction—when more people share their preferences. That is, I have documented phenomena analogous to the tyranny of the majority in markets. These findings stand in stark contrast to the notion that markets avoid objectionable features of collective choice.

My goal in this work is not so much to argue that Friedman is wrong. To the extent that Friedman is arguing that capitalism allows better tailoring of consumption opportunities to heterogeneous preferences than, say, a communist system of state-run industry, he is surely correct. Rather, my goal is to demonstrate that Friedman's dichotomy between markets and collective choice is not right. Under some simple circumstances that prevail in many markets, what I get depends on how many others also want it. Market allocation shares many of the features of allocation through collective choice. This finding—which is the chief message of the book—undermines some of the rationale to let the market decide such a wide array of questions.

When I first began talking about these ideas in seminars in the late 1990s, one prominent economist told me, "That's interesting. But aren't you worried about what the Right would do with those results?" This economist was presumably concerned that conservatives would see in the results an argument for promoting residential segregation. For example, clusters of blacks would bring forth products more appealing to blacks, relieving pressure for policies promoting residential mobility by minorities. A week later, another prominent economist had a similar but opposite reaction, finding it "interesting" but expressing concern about "what the Left would do with the results." This economist was presumably concerned that activists would see an argument for subsidizing products targeted at minorities and other small groups of consumers. Annoying people across the ideological spectrum confirmed my sense that I was on to something. This book is the result.

This book is the distilled product of ten years of work, much of it undertaken with students and colleagues, to whom I am enormously grateful. Collaborators who helped educate me include Steve Berry, Lisa George, Felix Oberholzer-Gee, Peter Siegelman, and Todd Sinai. I have benefited from comments on the book draft from my editor at Harvard University Press, Mike Aronson, as well as Mary Benner, Steve Berry, Matt Kahn, Jeff Milyo, Fiona Scott-Morton, Asher Waldfogel, and two anonymous referees.

I am grateful for the intellectual atmosphere of the Wharton School, where I have been free to pursue empirical applied economics informed by heavy doses of reality. I am also grateful for the hospitality of the Wharton Marketing Department during a leave in the fall of 2005, when I completed a draft of the manuscript.

This book is dedicated to three sets of people who have been instrumental in my life and work: my wife, Mary Benner, an accomplished scholar who has supported this project from before its beginning; my father, Melvin, and late mother, Gertrude, whose rearing made me sensitive to the concerns of preference minorities; and my children, Hannah and Sarah, who inspire me every day.

The Tyranny of the Market

Introduction

Societies need to make decisions about material questions, such as what to produce and who gets what; broadly, these decisions can be made either through political processes such as voting or through voluntary arrangements among individuals in markets. Choices made through voting result in "laws" that apply to everyone. Whatever decision the group makes, everyone must obey. Laws have some disadvantages, which can be illustrated by an imaginary town meeting. Will the town square be a playground or a shopping mall? Only one outcome is possible; the space cannot be both. Suppose that 55 percent of the people want the shopping mall. After three hours of impassioned speeches by parents of small children, who want the playground, and shoppers, who want the mall, there is a vote. The mall wins, and the town square will become a mall. After the meeting, 55 percent of the voters go home happy, while the other 45 percent go home dissatisfied. With majority rule, those in the majority are winners, while those in the minority are losers. This is an example of what the nineteenth-century English political philosopher John Stuart Mill called the "tyranny of the majority." With some questions—will abortion be legal, how much will we spend on national defense—society must come to a single answer. Unless all people agree, the answer will upset some, and there will be tyranny of the majority.

A dominant strand of current thinking holds that markets are distinctly different from, and superior to, government as means of allocation. Markets are thought to avoid the tyranny of the majority because in markets each person can decide what she wants. Milton Friedman's 1962 landmark book *Capitalism and Freedom* puts it this way: the "characteristic feature of action through political channels is that it tends to require or enforce substantial conformity. The great advantage of the market, on the other hand, is that it permits wide diversity. It is, in political terms, a system of proportional representation. Each man can vote, as it were, for the color of tie he wants and get it; he does not have to see what color the majority wants and then, if he is in the minority, submit" (p. 15).

The statement that "each man can vote . . . for the color of the tie he wants and get it" bears repeating. It is a statement that what's available to me in markets depends only on my preferences, not on anyone else's. This rationale has stood for years as a compelling argument bolstering calls to "let the market decide" a wide variety of questions and for moving allocation decisions outside of the messy political sphere, where others' preferences inhibit my options, and into the pure economic one. But do markets really liberate consumers from their neighbors' tastes? And do they avoid problems akin to tyranny of the majority that are endemic to allocation through government?

An extended example raises some questions: Try driving across the United States with only a car radio for entertainment. In remote locations you may receive no radio stations at all. As you drive through small towns, you will receive a few stations, perhaps one broadcasting country music and another airing "fire and brimstone" religious programming. Scanning the dial as you drive through an urban area of one million people, you will find twenty to twenty-five stations broadcasting in about fifteen distinct programming formats, including Top 40, oldies, adult contemporary, classic rock, alternative rock, and perhaps jazz and classical. When you get to New York or Los Angeles, you will be able to receive as many as fifty different radio stations. In short, larger markets support more—and generally a wider variety—of products. More people will find an option they find attractive when more products are available. In this sense, people benefit each other in markets by helping to make additional products profitable and therefore available. Yet it is clear that in this market, as when voting, my preferences alone do not determine what's available to me.

There is more to the story than a simple bigger-is-better argument, however. Suppose you prefer radio programming in Spanish. Remote locations will offer you no options in either English or Spanish. As you tour the country, you will find Spanish-language programming in most major urban areas, but the places with the most Spanish programming will not be the largest urban areas. Rather you will find the greatest variety of Spanish-language stations in the metro areas with the largest Hispanic populations. The McAllen-Brownsville, Texas, area, for example, with an overall population of about 650,000 in 1997, had seventeen local radio stations, eight of them broadcasting in Spanish. By contrast, the Tulsa, Oklahoma, metro area, roughly equal in size, had twenty-one local stations, all of them broadcasting in English. This comparison demonstrates that your satisfaction as a consumer depends not simply on market size but more specifically on the number of persons who share your preferences. I call this the "who benefits whom" phenomenon. By making it profitable for firms to offer more Spanish-language stations, additional Hispanics benefit other Hispanics. But, as in this example, they need not benefit English speakers, and English speakers need not benefit them.

These simple examples challenge the supposed stark distinction between markets and collective choice. Listeners' options on the radio dial, and their ensuing satisfaction with those options, depend not only on their preferences, but also on the prevalence of their preferences in the potential market. You will find products that suit you only if enough others also want the product. If you are alone, or nearly alone, in your preference for some product, it will not be made available. This mechanism is a mild market analogue to the widely acknowledged tyranny of the majority in voting.

The "who benefits whom" phenomenon is by no means confined to radio broadcast markets. Let's rejoin the cross-country driving tour. Suppose you like Afghan food, and your traveling companion likes hamburgers. Because many Americans like hamburgers, your friend will find appealing options essentially anywhere there is sufficient population concentration to support a restaurant. You, by contrast, will find an appealing Afghan option only in huge cities, because these cities are the only places with enough fans of Afghan cuisine to make an Afghan restaurant profitable. Your friend will always find satisfaction at mealtime, while you rarely will. Substitute kosher, halal, peanut-allergic, or Vietnamese for Afghan as your culinary preference, and you can tell a similar story.

So far it's clear that you can be better off in your capacity as a consumer of a particular product as more consumers share your preferences. The situation outlined is not a tyranny of the majority per se. You are helped by additional persons who agree with you; and while persons with different preferences do not help you, they do not harm you either. But the story need not end here. Think of product categories such as daily newspapers, in which there are very few products per metropolitan area, and often just one. In this case, the single product can be positioned to appeal to one group or another. As one group grows larger, the product moves toward the growing group to suit its needs and attract more of them as buyers. This shift makes members of the growing group better off, but members of the other group worse off, since the product is moving further from what they like. If there is a single product whose appeal depends on its positioning, then consumers are better off as more people agree with them and worse off as more people disagree. Not only do more people with my tastes help me, but also more people with different preferences can hurt me. This is the tyranny of the market, the product-market analogue to the conventional tyranny of the majority in voting. Just as the minority leaves the town meeting unhappy with the majority choice, people whose ideal product is far from the sole product's positioning are hurt by others with different preferences.

This argument is not just about obscure or unimportant markets or about hypothetical or arbitrary groups (such as Afghan food lovers). Instead, only two broad features are required for markets to share the fractious features of allocation through politics, in which groups are pitted one against another. First, preferences must differ across groups. And second, something—generally fixed costs—must limit the number of available options and prevent products from being provided to small groups of potential buyers.

The United States has been described as a "melting pot," as a nation of immigrants, as a pluralistic society. Whatever one's preferred metaphor, the United States surely has a diverse population of people with different preferences about many policies and products. About 13 percent of the 275 million persons in the United States are black, and 13 percent are Hispanic.[1] As I will document later, preferences for many products differ sharply between blacks and whites and between Hispanics and non-Hispanics. In the standard view of the economy, people of diverse preferences would find what they want regardless of the popularity of their choices. But if the view I am advancing in this book is correct, then blacks, Hispanics, and other "preference minorities"—that is, small groups of people with atypical preferences—will see fewer appealing products and will be less satisfied than the majority as consumers and as citizens.

Anyone can be a preference minority. Most people have unusual tastes in some products, say for butter-brickle ice cream or for grapefruit-flavored soft drinks. But some preference minorities can be defined before the fact by ethnicity, culture, or biology—factors that can lead to different product needs. For these ex ante preference minorities, preferences may be less of an elective choice than for those preferring butter brickle. For example, Hispanics speak a different language than most other people in the United States, leading to a preference for media products in Spanish. Orthodox Jews and Muslims have dietary rules that give rise to a strong preference not to eat pork. Celiacs cannot consume gluten, giving rise to very different food needs. People with peanut or seafood allergies also prefer different foods. In all of these cases, the word "preference" is an understatement, since it implies more choice than may be feasible.

The main point of this book is that the supposed dichotomy between markets and politics is not generally correct. While there are some circumstances in which one's satisfaction does not depend on other consumers' preferences—so that the dichotomy between markets and politics holds—there are many important situations in which one consumer's satisfaction does depend on others. In these markets—as in politics—the happiness of consumers will depend not just on their own preferences, but also on the prevalence of their preferences. In short, the market does not generally avoid the tyranny of the majority. In spite of the liberation rhetoric often used to describe the market, the same kinds of groups disadvantaged by majority rule—small groups with different preferences—can find themselves at a disadvantage in product markets as well. This raises a challenge to the common exhortation "Let the market decide."

The first part of this book lays out the ideas. Chapter 1 describes, with intuitive examples, the circumstances in which markets produce effects similar to the tyranny of the majority. These effects include more (or more appealing) products for larger consumer groups, greater consumer satisfaction for larger groups, and in some instances harmful effects of one group's size on the satisfaction of other groups of consumers. Chapter 2 asks whether the fact that markets can share features of political allocation is, on close inspection, undesirable. When fixed costs are large and preferences differ across consumers, do markets achieve desirable outcomes? Are they efficient? Are they fair?

Part II presents empirical evidence on several specific industries that share the features of large fixed costs and preferences that differ across consumers. Using blacks and whites, and Hispanics and non-Hispanics, as groups, and pointing to local media markets as a major example, I show, first, that preferences differ sharply across groups. Second, I demonstrate that product targeting is sensitive to group size. Finally, I document that consumption, and satisfaction with the products, is higher as groups are larger. Chapter 3 illustrates the "who benefits whom" phenomenon with evidence on radio broadcasting and illustrates the more extreme tyranny of the majority with data on the daily newspaper industry. Chapter 4 shows that the "who benefits whom" phenomenon also operates at the neighborhood level in the restaurant industry.

For many products, consumption is an end in itself. For others, including information products such as newspapers and broadcasting, consumption is a means to other ends, such as knowing how and whether to participate in civic affairs. Chapter 5 provides an important extension on how the availability of group-targeted media products affects whether the targeted individuals vote. The chapters of Part II collectively show that just as my welfare as a citizen is limited by my neighbors' political preferences, my welfare as a consumer is limited by my neighbors' product preferences. Moreover, my neighbors' preferences for media products affect how easily I can become informed, a process that reinforces the political advantage of large groups.

Having outlined the problem—that markets share features of collective choice—I move in Part III to a discussion of possible solutions. The most obvious market-based solution to a problem created by large fixed costs in relation to market size is larger markets. Products created for a national rather than a local market, and that are "traded" across regions, allow a test for whether market size is a liberating force. Chapter 6 shows that trade is a liberating force for isolated consumers. The Internet and cable television are illustrative examples of new technologies that allow information trading across places, thereby increasing the number of other like-minded consumers who can support products that each person prefers. For example, blacks in more predominantly white metropolitan areas use the Internet more than less-isolated blacks, showing that market enlargement provides some liberation from neighbors' tastes.

But the extent of liberation available from larger markets is limited. Larger markets generally beget more (and more varied) products, but in some industries, larger markets beget products that are bigger and better for many but not all consumers. Chapter 7 illustrates these possibilities using the contrast between the restaurant industry, where the quantity and variety of products grows with the size of the market, and the daily newspaper industry, where the size rather than the number of products grows with market size. Chapter 8 examines some subtleties that arise with trade in high fixed cost products. Although trade generally increases the number of options available to consumers, trade can also cause a repositioning of products, bringing about a "tyranny of alien majorities." For example, imported products can draw customers from local products, forcing local products to reposition if they are to continue covering fixed costs. This can benefit some consumers while harming others. Chapter 9 discusses technological changes as a source of liberation, with a series of examples.

Parts II and III provide empirical evidence that market allocation shares some of the objectionable features of collective choice. Even if markets are imperfect, it is not always clear whether the alternatives would be better. Part IV presents some discussion of policy responses to perceived shortcomings in markets. Chapter 10 reviews U.S. policies to subsidize the provision of high fixed cost products to small populations, including air transport, radio broadcasting, telecommunications, electricity, and pharmaceutical products. Chapter 11 provides a direct comparison of market and government provision of two products (books and liquor), both widely distributed by both government entities and private firms. The chapter then brings up the question of what sort of consumers benefit from the decision to allocate through markets rather than through government.

Please note that most of the chapters of the book are based on academic articles published in leading economics journals. Economic theory guides the questions, and systematic analysis of data allows the questions to be answered. To make the book as readable as possible, I have omitted much of the technical discussion. A reader interested in technical arcana is encouraged to consult the underlying academic articles, which are cited at places that invoke their arguments or evidence.

PART ONE

THEORY

CHAPTER 1

Markets and the Tyranny
of the Majority

This book is about "differentiated products": products like Coke and Pepsi that are similar but not identical. Many people can tell the difference and prefer one over the other. In automobiles the distinctions are more obvious. While both deliver motorized transportation on four wheels, a Humvee and a VW Beetle are quite different. Examples of differentiated products abound: automobiles, packaged foods, pharmaceuticals, information products (books, music, movies, newspapers, video programming), furniture, housing, consumer electronics, and clothing. Essentially, everything available at the mall, and most of the products outside the produce section of the grocery store, are differentiated products.[1]

I am concerned about people's access to differentiated products, such as books, restaurant meals, movies, and cars, that are well suited to their tastes. There are entire cottage industries devoted to critiquing products: think of restaurant, movie, and theater critics. Major newspapers provide weekly columns with critical descriptions and side-by-side comparisons of new technological gadgets. And, of course, *Consumer Reports* produces a monthly magazine, as well as many annual reference publications, comparing features of cars, appliances, and a host of other consumer products. These popular sources are interesting to many readers who want to know whether this or that product is well suited to their tastes and needs.

13

How well do markets provide products that appeal to a diverse array of consumers? To analyze this question we need to take a slightly technical detour to develop a way of characterizing differentiation. The detour takes us through a "model" of differentiated products. A model is a simplified description of reality that, if it captures the important features, can be used to understand how the world works. Significantly, a model's predictions are not the same as evidence. Instead, they tell us what sort of evidence to look for.

A model requires some assumptions about both products and the behaviors of buyers and sellers. While products differ in many ways, assume that products differing in a single way can be represented on a line between zero and one hundred.[2] For example, think of shirts that are identical except in color, and the points on the line segment are points on the color spectrum running from red to violet.[3]

Second, suppose that each potential consumer has a favorite shirt color somewhere along the line and likes shirts of other colors less the more they differ from his favorite color. Each consumer buys his most preferred shirt among those available. Third, suppose that there are a thousand consumers spaced evenly, or "uniformly," along the line. That is, there are just as many consumers whose favorite color is a particular shade of red as there are consumers favoring a particular shade of blue. Third, offering shirts for sale in a particular color entails a setup, or "fixed," cost, plus a per-shirt "variable" cost, for labor and materials. Anyone can enter as a seller and offer as many varieties as she wants, provided she first pays the fixed, or setup, cost for each color offered.

Finally, suppose that fixed costs are $100 for each color that a seller offers, variable costs for labor and materials are $15 per shirt, and the price of shirts is held constant at $20.[4] Then what does the market outcome look like? By our assumption that everyone buys a shirt, we know that people will buy 1,000 shirts at $20 each. Of the resulting $20,000 in industry revenue, $15,000 covers variable costs, leaving $5,000 to cover fixed costs (of providing different color offerings) as well as any profit.

How many varieties can the market support? With $5,000 available after covering variable costs, the market can sustain up to 50 varieties, evenly spaced along the line (at 1, 3, 5, . . . , 99). Each seller gets all of the customers within one segment on either side. For example, the seller at 1 gets all customers from 0 to 2, which is 2 percent of the 1,000 customers, or twenty customers. Revenue from those twenty customers totals $400, of which $300 is used to pay for raw materials, and the remaining $100 covers the setup costs exactly. In this scenario there is little effect of other people's preferences on the appeal of my best available option. True, consumers whose favorite color is at location 1 along the line get exactly what they want while consumers at, say, 2 do not. But every buyer gets an option within a distance of 1 of his most preferred color.

What happens if fixed costs are higher, say $1,000? Then with the $5,000 left over after the sellers cover variable costs, the market can sustain at most only five color varieties evenly spaced along the spectrum (at 10, 30, 50, 70, and 90). This is the first important insight: as fixed costs rise, the number of varieties available in the market declines. We have assumed that everyone keeps buying, but customers are not as happy as they were with more options. The average distance between their favorite color and the color they buy shows their dissatisfaction. With 50 colors available, the average distance is 0.5; with 5, it's 5. Everyone still gets a shirt, but it's now typically a color they like much less.

Whether this market brings forth products close to consumers' ideals depends on the magnitude of fixed costs. If fixed costs are high, then there are relatively few products spaced far apart. In that case, the product space is "lumpy," with products few and far between. The lower are fixed costs, the more product varieties the market will offer. If there are no fixed costs, then there is no limit to the number of options available in this hypothetical example, and each consumer is free to choose a product that exactly matches his ideal. The product space is then "smooth," in the sense that it is filled with products of every conceivable type.

So far, although we have customers getting less happy as fixed costs rise, we have no "who benefits whom" or "tyranny of the majority" phenomena because we have no distinction among the types of customers. Preferences differ across consumers, but only via the uniform distribution of favorite colors along the line. There are equal numbers of consumers preferring each color, so there are no identifiable clusters of consumers and no preference minorities.

Suppose, instead, that there are two distinct groups of customers. Because much of the evidence in later chapters concerns preferences that differ by race, let's simply call them "blacks" and "whites" even though we know nothing about how preferences over shirt colors differ by race. Suppose that blacks' favorite colors are uniformly distributed over the range 0–20, while whites' favorite colors are uniformly distributed over the range 20–100. Let's say there are 100 blacks in the population and 900 whites. There are still 1,000 consumers total, so that if fixed costs are $100, the market can again accommodate 50 shirt varieties. For viability, each product must have 20 customers for which it is the nearest color. Where will sellers locate their products? In the 0–20 region (where blacks' preferred colors lie), sellers will locate 4 units apart (at 2, 6, 10, 14, and 18).[5] From 20 to 100 the market can accommodate more varieties per consumer. On average, then, white-targeted varieties will locate 1.77 units from each other. As a result, since whites get shirts closer to their desired colors, their satisfaction with the market is greater than blacks'. This example illustrates what I term the "who benefits whom" phenomenon: the more that people share my preferences, the more that markets will supply me with products that I find appealing.

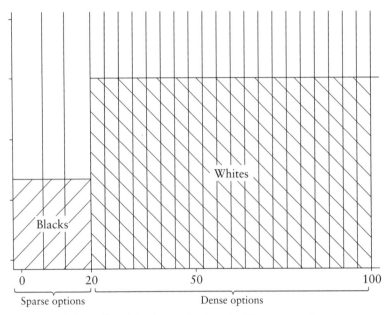

Colors offered by the market (vertical lines are options)

FIGURE 1. Products targeting large and small groups with different preferences. This figure shows how many people prefer each color, as well as the locations of available products. Here the color spectrum runs from 0 to 100. Vertical lines show the location of products, which are shirts of different colors. Horizontal lines indicate the relative numbers of people of each type. In this hypothetical scenario, black people, who constitute 10 percent of the population, prefer colors between 0 and 20, while white people prefer colors between 20 and 100. As a result, shirt varieties are more plentiful between 20 and 100 than between 0 and 20.

Figure 1 illustrates the situation. The 100 black consumers are distributed evenly between 0 and 20, and the products targeting them are located at the vertical lines between 0 and 20. The 900 whites' favorite shirt colors are distributed uniformly between 20 and 100. Whites' demand is denser across all of the white-preferred colors (11.25 = 900/80 versus 5 = 100/20); as a result, white-targeted products are more plentiful.

Thus far I have shown how the number of products targeting each group, and each group's satisfaction from consuming the available products, can increase with its own size and decrease as fixed costs are higher. In the examples to this point, group members help each other with increases in group size, but they do not harm members of the other group.

But an actual tyranny of the majority is possible in product markets. That is, more members of one group can actually harm members of the other group. When fixed costs become high enough so that the market supplies only one variety, the question becomes: where will this product locate? Location matters because consumers are more satisfied as the product is closer to their favorite. To add a layer of realism, suppose that consumers will purchase only if the product is "close enough" to their favorite color. Then the firm's targeting decision affects its revenue.[6]

Suppose there are two groups: 500 "red" persons with favorites distributed uniformly between 0 and 50, and another 500 "violet" persons with favorite colors distributed uniformly between 50 and 100. If the tendency for a customer to purchase the product declines as the product is farther from his favorite, then a single variety cannot do any better than locating at 50, the location that minimizes the distance to the farthest customer (see Fig. 2).

How does this change if the red population remains 500, while the violet population increases to 750? If the tendency to purchase declines with distance to the favorite, the best location for the single product must move toward violet (to the right). For example, if people buy only if the product is within 10 units of their favorite, then the best the seller can do is to locate somewhere between 60 and 90 (see Fig. 3). The growth in the violet-preferring population makes the single product available less appealing to the reds. The

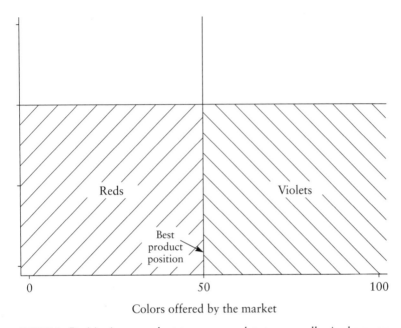

FIGURE 2. Positioning a product to accommodate two equally sized groups with different preferences. With equally sized groups of two types of consumers, the reds (between 0 and 50) and the violets (between 50 and 100), the best a single product's seller can do is to locate at 50 (halfway between 0 and 100).

key point here is that, with only one product in the market, an increase in the size of one group will not only tend to help the larger group; it can also harm the smaller group.

This is a startling statement. It is the tyranny of the majority translated almost literally from the realm of voting into the realm of markets. It is worth returning at this point to Friedman's argument that in markets, "each man can vote for the color of the tie that he wants and get it." If there are no fixed costs, then this is true. But if fixed costs are substantial, then this is not true.

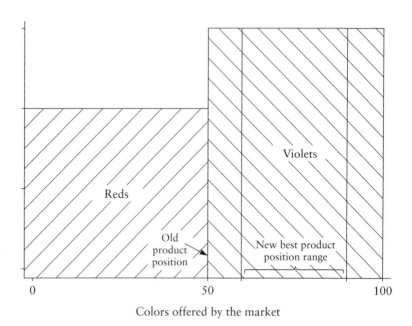

Colors offered by the market

FIGURE 3. Positioning a product to accommodate two differently sized groups with different preferences. The situation with a higher violet-preferring population is shown here by the higher horizontal line above a color of 50. Because consumers buy a shirt only if it is within 10 of their ideal color, the best color that the seller of the single shirt can chose is between 60 and 90.

Instead, a consumer is free to choose such products only if sufficiently many others also want them. And if fixed costs are high enough, then people who do not share my product preferences not only do not help me; they actually make me worse off in markets.

CHAPTER 2

Are "Lumpy" Markets a Problem?

When fixed costs are large relative to market size—when markets are "lumpy"—the number of options targeting each group, and their satisfaction, will increase as the size of the group grows. If fixed costs are very large, an increase in the size of one group can decrease the well-being of another group. For example, we expect preference minorities—small groups of consumers with tastes distinct from the tastes of the majority—to fare relatively poorly as consumers. Black Americans, for example, make up 13 percent of the U.S. population. As I will show in later chapters, as groups, blacks and whites have very different preferences. We would therefore expect product markets to deliver them less satisfaction. If documented, would these phenomena constitute a problem? Is this a defect of private markets? If so, would it warrant government intervention?

Before proceeding I should make clear that my argument about the satisfaction that markets deliver to preference minorities is entirely distinct from two conventional arguments about why various kinds of ethnic minority groups fare poorly in markets, discrimination and poverty. A great deal of research effort has been devoted to showing that ethnic and racial minorities suffer intentional discrimination at the hands of their fellow citizens. Discrimination can take a variety of forms, including lower pay for the same work or higher prices for the same products.[1] Here, by contrast, I demonstrate that the very workings of the market can deliver fewer products and less satisfaction to minorities, in circumstances when they are also preference minorities.

An extreme example makes the point obvious. Roughly 1 percent of the U.S. population is allergic to peanuts, and consuming them creates a life-threatening emergency.[2] The peanut-allergic constitute a preference minority, a small group with distinct preferences for peanut-free candy and cookies, in particular. Of the products at your nearby candy store, roughly half contain peanuts in at least trace amounts. Thus the peanut-allergic face fewer product alternatives. Unless they enjoy peanut-free snacks (such as taffies or caramels) more than nonallergic persons do, it is fair to suppose that peanut-allergic consumers get less satisfaction from the snack market. The reason is not discrimination. Candy and cookie makers do not dislike peanut-allergic customers. Rather, such customers do not make up a large enough market to warrant targeting more products at them. Because the fixed costs of offering a candy or cookie variety are relatively small, this is not an acute problem.[3] There are some products that appeal to peanut-allergic persons; there just aren't as many.

Nor, second, am I making the conventional argument about poverty that an individual with less money than others can purchase less. For a variety of historical reasons, including past discrimination, blacks typically have less money than their white counterparts. As a result, they are able to purchase less. My point, though, is not about how much people can buy but rather about how effectively the products that the market brings forth appeal to different sorts of people. If blacks and whites have different preferences for products with high fixed costs, then even a wealthy black person will not be "free to choose" products that appeal to him. Appealing products would be made available only if his demand, along with his compatriots', were sufficient to generate revenue in excess of the cost of supplying his preferred product. If few of his fellow consumers share his tastes, he will be an unfulfilled consumer regardless of his means.

Do the phenomena I am discussing—markets delivering less satisfaction to small groups—constitute shortcomings of market allocation? There are two possible reasons to care about the possibility that product markets deliver less satisfaction to some groups and, moreover, that people's satisfaction depends on others. First, in spite of what you may recall from Economics 101 (if you took it in college), market allocation need not be efficient. That is, real-world markets do not necessarily provide every product that offers benefits to society in excess of costs. Second, there are distributional concerns about who wins and who loses in markets.

Are Lumpy Markets Inefficient?

While perhaps distressing at some level, it is not necessarily inefficient for society to deliver fewer products that appeal to small groups. Efficiency dictates that a product should only be provided if its benefit to society—that is, the sum of benefits experienced by all its users—exceeds its cost of provision, including both the fixed setup costs and the variable costs of production. If fewer people prefer red than violet, then if per-product costs and per-consumer benefits are equal for the two colors, the total potential benefit of the red products can cover the costs of fewer red than violet products. In that sense, there in fact should be fewer red than violet products. Fewer products targeting small groups with distinct preferences may be socially desirable, at least in the sense of being efficient.

That said, when fixed costs are present, the market outcome is not necessarily efficient either. We want our economic system to guarantee that things that ought to get done do get done. How should we determine what should get done? The economist's standard way is to add up the maximum amounts that all consumers would be willing to pay for some good, then ask whether that aggregate valuation exceeds the cost of provision. If so, then the good should be provided.

A numerical example helps make this point clear. Suppose a firm is contemplating offering an entirely new product, for which no near substitutes currently exist. There are five potential consumers, whose valuations of this product are, in descending order, ten dollars, nine dollars, eight dollars, seven dollars, and six dollars. These are the maximum amounts that each of the consumers would be willing to pay for a unit of the new product. So, what is the availability of the new product worth to society? The answer is $40 ($10 + $9 + $8 + $7 + $6).

Whether the product should be provided depends on how its aggregate value to consumers ($40) compares with its cost of provision. Cost of provision can have both a fixed component as well as a marginal (or per-additional-unit) cost, for materials and labor. Whether the market does what should be done will depend crucially on the role of fixed costs. The larger are fixed costs, the less likely that the market can get it right. Suppose, first, that there is no fixed cost, while there is a constant $5 marginal cost (for each additional unit). Then provision of five units would cost $25 and benefit society $40. This product should be provided. Will it?

Whether a market brings forth that product depends on how the revenue that a private seller can get compares with cost, rather than how aggregate social valuation—the sum of consumers' willingness to pay—compares with cost. How much revenue is available to the seller? This depends on whether the seller can charge each buyer his maximum willingness to pay. In general, this is infeasible, because a person who can obtain the product for a low price can purchase all of the units and resell them, like a ticket-scalper, to people willing to pay more. The real-life market transaction that comes closest to the custom-pricing ideal is the determination of a family's tuition bill at elite U.S. colleges. Each family must fill out a detailed financial aid form indicating their ability to pay, and this process determines the family's customized price. Customized pricing works for college, because one's seat at school—and, more important, one's transcript—is not transferable to others.

Without customized pricing, what is the maximum revenue available in our example? To figure this out, imagine successively charging each price from $10 to $6 per unit. What would revenue be? At a price of $10, only one person would buy, generating revenue of $10. At a price of $9, two would buy, generating revenue of $18. At $8; $24. At $7; $28. At a price of $6, revenue reaches its "profit-maximizing" peak of $30; and with $5 marginal costs and no fixed costs, revenue exceeds the $25 total costs, and the market can make this product available.

If fixed costs are $20 rather than zero, then with this array of potential buyers, revenue ($30) does not exceed costs ($20 + $25 = $45), and the good is not provided. But with fixed costs of $20, the $40 in benefits do not exceed costs, and the product should not be provided. With very high fixed costs relative to demand, the product will not, and should not, be provided. This is the sense in which failure to provide is not necessarily inefficient.

But suppose that fixed costs are $10 instead of $20. The benefit of the product remains $40, while the total cost of providing five units is now $35 ($10 + $25). The product should therefore be provided, but the maximum revenue available to the firm, at least the firm that cannot successfully customize prices, is $30. Hence the market does not deliver the product, even though it should be provided.

What is going wrong when the product should be, but is not, provided? When there are fixed costs and firms cannot perfectly tailor prices to capture consumers' full valuation of products, then markets can fail to deliver things that should be provided. Whether this is a remote special case or a common occurrence depends on the technology of production, or whether the markets in question are lumpy or smooth. If typical industries have smooth cost structures—at the extreme, with purely marginal costs—then this problem will not generally arise. But if fixed costs are sizable, as they are in many industries, then markets may quite commonly fail to deliver products that should be provided.

When are such failures most acute? Inefficient underprovision is more acute as revenue more greatly understates consumer valuation. Suppose a small group of persons places a high valuation on a product, while most people place a lower value.[4] Then the best price the firm can charge will not capture the high-intensity consumers' valuation as revenue. In reality, then, where do we expect to find inefficient underprovision in markets? First, we expect it in industries whose cost structures have a large fixed component (and as explained later, fixed costs are in fact surprisingly widespread).

Second, we expect to find this underprovision where the number of relevant consumers is too small for revenue alone to cover costs. In the earlier example, with a price of $6 and a marginal cost of $5, each unit sold generated $1 of revenue in excess of marginal cost. With only five units sold, this excess amounts to only $5, which is shy of the $10 fixed cost. But if the market doubled in size to two each of the five consumer valuation types, then there would be ten units sold at $6 each, allowing the firm to cover its fixed costs exactly. The point here is that size mitigates the problem, which is just another view of the "who benefits whom" phenomenon. Consumers become "free to choose" a high fixed cost option only when enough fellow consumers also want it. If there are no fixed costs, then small groups face no disadvantages in product markets. If anyone is willing to pay in excess of the marginal cost of production, a seller can profitably offer the product. ("Each man can vote for the color of tie he wants and get it.") But when fixed costs are large, members of large groups will face more product options.

As a practical matter, where would we expect markets to get it wrong? As we will explore in more depth beginning in the next chapter, in markets of different sizes there will be a size threshold where the product is provided, defining the level of demand where revenue covers costs. In markets a shade smaller than those where provision occurs, it is likely that social valuation exceeds costs, even if revenue cannot, causing inefficient underprovision. To find these markets that are too small for market provision, we can consider places with medium-sized populations, as well as products that are of interest to groups that are locally small.

Inefficient underprovision—the failure to offer a product with social benefit above cost—is not the only possible inefficiency arising from lumpy markets. Perhaps ironically, while increased market size mitigates the problem of inefficient underprovision, it gives rise to the opposite possibility: excessive numbers of similar products. As demand increases beyond the level that makes one product (or firm) viable, the revenue available can make it profitable for multiple sellers to profitably offer the product, even if their offerings are identical. Additional entry beyond the first product seller is beneficial to consumers only inasmuch as it puts downward pressure on prices, putting the product in reach of more customers. But additional entry is also socially costly because the fixed costs of setting up production are now being incurred multiple times. At some point, entry can be excessive, in that additional entry raises production costs without changing the product's pricing to make it available to more people. A return to our shirt color spectrum illustrates the point. Suppose some particular location along the spectrum, say the location 32, has a large mass of 100 consumers. When setup costs are 20, the market can accommodate five identical products at this exact location, even though—unless prices fall with additional entry—one seller would be optimal (since additional offerings at the same location do not decrease any consumers' distance to the nearest product). Examples like this occur in the real world. In 1993, the Dallas metropolitan area had six country music radio stations with similar programming, all vying for the same listeners.[5]

When products are differentiated, additional offerings beyond the first can theoretically benefit society both by putting downward pressure on prices and by providing options closer to additional consumers' ideal products. But there is still no reason to expect the market outcome to be efficient.

Market Success, Market Failure, and the Gray Area Between

When we rely on private markets, in theory three different kinds of situations may arise: those where markets work perfectly (in the sense of doing all that should be done); those where markets may work (in the sense that some firms will be able to offer some products); and those where markets do not work at all. What in fact happens depends on the scale required for making the product as well as whether sellers can successfully charge buyers any part of their willingness to pay.

Strictly speaking, the only markets that work perfectly in theory are known as "perfectly competitive" markets. This is the economics profession's major gift to the world, shared largely through introductory college economics courses. Many economists also look to the lessons of the perfectly competitive model for advising policy makers. If you have taken a course in economics, you spent about half of the semester studying the perfectly competitive model, in which many sellers produce an identical product. Competition among them drives the cost of production to its lowest possible level, maximizing the joint welfare of producers and consumers. In a perfectly competitive market, everything that should get done does without government involvement. And government regulation can only make society worse off. This is the model invoked to show the wasteful effects of rent control, agricultural subsidies, and trade restrictions on goods produced in perfectly competitive markets.

To arrive at this point, you are first taught "consumer theory," whose main and largely unobjectionable lesson is that people buy more of an item, and experience more satisfaction as consumers, when its price is lower. So reliable is this relationship that it is venerated as the Law of Demand. The area under the market demand curve—which indicates how much people collectively want to buy at any price—shows the social benefit of the product.

Second, you are taught "producer theory," which concerns how firms make their products with raw materials. An industry can accommodate many firms only under particular assumptions about production. In the standard textbook story about production, there is an optimal scale for every firm producing a product. Fixed costs help determine the optimal scale: higher fixed costs lead to higher optimal scale. If the optimal scale is small relative to market demand, then the industry accommodates many firms. For example, if industry output is one million units per year, and a firm can achieve low costs producing, say, one thousand units of output, then there might be one thousand firms in the industry. Then the market is, effectively, perfectly competitive. At the extreme, this situation corresponds to our earlier examples in which there were no fixed costs.

At the other extreme from goods whose conditions give rise to perfectly competitive—and perfectly functioning—markets are what are known as "public goods." Public goods have the feature that users cannot be excluded from using the good if it is made available for anyone. As a result, a person trying to sell the good will not get paid except through the goodwill of some customers. National defense is the classic example. Imagine Lockheed Martin going door-to-door asking households to pay for their share of the Star Wars missile shield, assuming—for the sake of discussion—that the shield is a worthwhile project. It's essentially like trying to sell the Brooklyn Bridge. Whether the household pays or not, they will get the benefit of the shield if the shield goes up, just as the Brooklyn Bridge will continue to span the East River whether they "buy" it or not. So people get no direct benefit from contributing. Of course, if no one pays, then Lockheed Martin cannot deploy the shield. But with over a hundred million households in the nation, the probability that one family's decision to pay will make the project viable is nil. So, unless they are altruistic—or gullible, in the case of the bridge—people will not contribute. And the project does not get provided, even if it has value in excess of its cost.

Such a situation represents downright market failure. A project worth doing does not get done when left to private voluntary action by free individuals ("the market"). Doing it requires government action, and observers at all points on the political spectrum agree that this is a proper activity of government.[6]

There are other situations understood, by a broad spectrum of observers, to produce market failure. Two important examples involve "externalities" and "asymmetric information." Suppose I have a factory that produces a useful item that I sell to customers. In the course of making the product, however, I pollute the air. My total cost of making the product understates the cost to society, since my firm does not pay for the air I damage during manufacture (the "externality"). Because my direct money costs of making the product understate the total costs to society, I charge too little, and—because of the Law of Demand—people consume too much. This is a situation in which the market, left to itself, does not produce an efficient result. The price is too low, and consumption is too high.[7]

Asymmetric information refers to a situation when, say, the seller knows more about a product than the buyer. The paradigmatic example is used cars. There is a saying that a car depreciates 10 percent the moment its buyer drives it off the new car lot. Why might this be? Cars are complicated machines. It is difficult for most buyers to know, prior to purchase, whether this particular vehicle is a "lemon." The seller, however, has some experience with the car. He drives it every day and knows whether it starts reliably, whether it burns oil, and so on. Given that some fraction of the cars out there are lemons, what might a savvy buyer infer from the fact that the current owner wants to sell? He figures that the seller has a lemon he wants to unload. This is why ads for used cars often contain fabricated reasons for selling that are ostensibly unrelated to the car. "I'm moving to New York City, where I'll use the subway." "Trans Am. Belonged to my grandmother, who recently died."

The serious effect of asymmetric information, however, is that when buyers cannot determine the quality of the items they buy prior to purchase, they are not willing to pay top dollar. Given this, sellers do not bring best-quality items to market, reinforcing the problem. Given this vicious cycle, in the end "the bad drives out the good," and generally only low-quality items can be transacted if there is asymmetric information.[8]

Asymmetric information is a problem with both market and regulatory solutions. One private solution is warranties. A used car dealer can promise satisfaction or money back within thirty days. This amount of time allows the buyer to come to know everything that the seller knows about the car. Given that the buyer could return the car if unsatisfied, the seller has little incentive to misrepresent the actual quality of the car. Through "lemon laws"—which may mandate, for example, that a dealer must accept a return for thirty days after sale—governments can compel sellers to offer warranties.

Houses are easily as complicated as cars. Because of this, state laws require sellers to disclose large amounts of information about the houses to potential sellers. Has it ever had termite or water damage? And so on. Without such disclosure, it is possible that the housing market would not work.

But the issues raised here are far more widespread than in the automobile and housing markets. Between the cases that work perfectly and those that don't work at all lies much of the economy. One reason is that for many industries, fixed costs are substantial. If fixed costs are large, then a market can accommodate few firms. If a market can accommodate only one, then it is a monopoly. The existence of one firm, or only a few, interferes with the market's ability to drive costs down toward the minimum cost of production. If products differ across firms (think shirts, from Chapter 1), then having only a few firms also means having few of the possible colors of shirts available. Whose favorite shirt colors get made? Yours? Mine? The favorite of a typical person?

Milton Friedman, perhaps the most prominent advocate of free markets, groups these situations with few firms or products under the general heading of monopoly and grants that this is a problem. "The existence of monopoly means a limitation on voluntary exchange through a reduction in the alternatives available to individuals."[9] Although the conditions for perfect competition would seem to limit the number of situations in which it occurs, Friedman argues that the perfectly competitive model provides a reasonable approximation of many real-world industries.

> Of course, competition is an ideal type, like a Euclidean line—which has zero width and depth—yet we all find it useful to regard many a Euclidean volume—such as a surveyor's string—as a Euclidean line. Similarly, there is no such thing as "pure" competition. Every producer has some effect, however tiny, on the price of the product he produces. The important issue for understanding and for policy is whether the effect is significant or can properly be neglected, as the surveyor can neglect the thickness of what he calls a "line." The answer must, of course, depend on the problem. But as I have studied economic activities in the United States, I have become increasingly impressed with how wide a range of problems and industries for which it is appropriate to treat the economy as if it were competitive.[10]

Yet the question of whether fixed costs are large enough to inhibit broad application of the perfectly competitive model cannot be resolved by theory alone. If fixed costs are substantial, there will be few products in a market; and larger markets will support more products. If fixed costs are negligible, then the number of products in a market will not depend on the number of potential buyers. If the conditions for perfect competition held literally, then each person would be free to choose among all of the product options he might want, and all persons would be similarly well served by markets, regardless of what others prefer. But as we will see, people are not similarly well served by many markets.

Fairness: Markets and Politics

We have seen that with high fixed costs, the adverse market outcomes experienced by preference minorities need not be efficient. The experiences of preference minorities are also arguably unfair.

Until recently fairness was a topic outside economists' worldview. After all, what is fair? Equal division of everything? Each according to his need? But recently, economists have started studying fairness, asking, in particular, whether people would prefer to share.[11] In some experiments, subjects have been paired, then one of them is offered some money and a choice between keeping all of it or sharing some of it with the partner. A large number of subjects prefer to share, even with a partner they've never met before. In other experiments, pairs of subjects have been asked to play an "ultimatum game." One subject is given, say, ten dollars. He must decide how much of the sum to offer to his partner. If the partner accepts the offer, then each party keeps his money. That is, if he offers the partner four dollars, and if she accepts it, then he gets six dollars and she gets four dollars. If she rejects the offer, however, neither party keeps anything. A substantial fraction of players offer their partners half. And a substantial fraction of people offered something, but less than half, reject the offer, making themselves worse off just to punish the proposer.[12] That is, many people would rather have nothing than less than half.

Similar behavior arises in high-stakes games outside the laboratory. This was illustrated, amusingly, when in 2002–2003 the Game

Show Network aired a show called *Friend or Foe,* in which six strangers become three pairs of contestants who are asked trivia questions. If the pair could agree on an answer and it was correct, they would get $500 or $1,000 per correct answer. At the end of each of three rounds of questions, the lowest-scoring team was asked to leave the show. Before leaving they had to play a game to divide their winnings, which could be as much as $22,000 and which averaged $2,800. They divided the pot by playing a game much like the games played in economics experiments. Without knowing what the other player would choose, each player had to choose to be a "friend" or a "foe." If both players chose "friend," they split the pot evenly. If both chose "foe," neither got anything. If one chose "foe" and he other chose "friend," the player choosing "foe" kept the whole pot.

Suppose the pot is $1,000, and a player ("Joe") is interested only in money. What should he do? If his partner/opponent ("Sue") chooses "friend," then Joe gets $500 for choosing "friend" but $1,000 for choosing "foe." Suppose Sue chooses "foe." Then Joe gets nothing either way. So Joe should play "foe" to get more money: It either doubles his payoff or has no effect. *Friend or Foe* lasted 105 episodes, so 630 people had the opportunity to make this decision, dividing a total of nearly one million dollars. Despite the monetary advantages of playing "foe," contestants played "friend" half the time, regardless of the stakes involved. People playing "friend" are, by their behavior, willing to risk giving up half the pot in order to divide the pot evenly. This example vividly illustrates that people care about fairness, at least when they're on television.

What does this have to do with high fixed cost product markets? It is arguably not fair if large groups face more or better options than small groups in product markets. If people dislike unequal divisions of game show rewards, they may also dislike markets that provide different product options to different sorts of consumers.

Think, for example, of uniform postal pricing in the United States. Postal patrons pay the same amount to mail a letter to any U.S. destination, no matter how remote. Fairness concerns, as much as efficiency, may explain this policy, as well as other policy responses to the preference minorities' conditions.

Is Government Intervention Warranted?

As we have seen, market outcomes can fall short of ideal outcomes, for either efficiency or fairness reasons. In those situations it is possible in principle for nonmarket institutional arrangements to deliver better outcomes. Does that mean that government intervention is warranted? Not necessarily. Just as markets can fail to achieve efficient results, government action can fail to achieve desirable results, for essentially four reasons.[13] First, allocation through government entails the tyranny of the majority directly. The main point of this book is that allocation through markets can entail effects akin to the tyranny of the majority that occurs through voting. If effects "akin to the tyranny of the majority" are a problem, then the actual tyranny of the majority inherent in allocation through government will be a problem too.[14]

Second, as various scholars have argued, regulatory activity can become "captured" by the very industries it seeks to regulate.[15] While a regulatory authority may be established to protect consumers from, say, high prices charged by airlines, the regulatory body may come, over time, to protect the interests of the industry itself.

Third, lacking a profit motive, governmental organizations providing products to consumers may face less pressure to be efficient. A private firm keeps its profits, which are the excess of its revenue over its costs. Notwithstanding the problems with firms outside of perfectly competitive contexts—that they may charge high prices, or make the wrong range of products—these firms still have every incentive to minimize their costs of production. In other words, private firms have every incentive to produce efficiently, whereas governmental bodies may not. Studies documenting cost reductions following privatization of state-owned enterprises provide some evidence that the concern is valid.[16] Fourth, governments can be corrupt.[17]

Recently scholars and policymakers have placed great focus on possible shortcomings of government involvement in resource allocation, giving rise to an understanding that the shortcomings in market allocation are not a reason to instead use government. At the same time, many economists and policymakers have encouraged great faith in markets. Markets have many well-understood benefits, and government has many well-understood difficulties. My goal here is to provide evidence about how many markets actually work, in contexts where they are understood to work well, so that policy makers and citizens can weigh the respective shortcomings of markets and government to determine an appropriate mix in each arena.

PART TWO

EMPIRICAL EVIDENCE

CHAPTER 3

Who Benefits Whom
in Practice

According to some estimates, it costs an average of $900 million to bring a prescription drug to market.[1] This is a fixed cost, independent of the number of doses sold. As a result, when a pharmaceutical company contemplates developing a drug, one major consideration is the size of the market. How many people have the condition and are in a position to pay for the drug?

Conditions afflicting large numbers of people in rich countries are targeted by the most products. As an article in the *New York Times* put it, "The pharmaceutical industry invests $27 billion a year in research, but most of that is a hunt for drugs to lengthen or brighten the lives of consumers who are already relatively healthy. Among the biggest sellers are drugs to grow hair, relieve impotence or fight cholesterol, ulcers, depressions, anxiety, allergies, arthritis and high blood pressure."[2] For example, there are nine different products available to treat acid reflux disease, which affects over half of the U.S. population annually (and a fifth weekly).[3] There are two major drugs to treat erectile dysfunction, affecting 15 to 30 million U.S. persons. And there are at least seven major drugs to treat allergy symptoms, which affect 40 million people in the United States. Conditions afflicting small populations often cannot attract drug companies' investment in developing a treatment. Indeed, there are no treatments available to treat most of the six thousand "orphan" conditions affecting fewer than 200,000 people each.[4]

It is clear that if you are going to be sick, you are better off having an illness that affects many rich people because you will be able to choose from many products with potential therapeutic benefit. If your disease affects few people, however, or few who can pay, then markets will provide few or no options. One vivid example of this is sleeping sickness in Africa. Sleeping sickness is a terrible disease transmitted by the bite of the tsetse fly. Over 300,000 people are infected each year. The disease causes "episodes of fever, headache, sweating" and its victims eventually fall into terminal comas.[5] A known medication, Eflornithine, can cure the illness. Developed as a cancer drug by an American subsidiary of Aventis, Eflornithine was by chance discovered to be highly effective against advanced sleeping sickness.[6] "It proved so spectacular at pulling people out of their final comas that it was nicknamed 'the Resurrection Drug.'"[7] Yet Aventis abandoned the drug when it proved ineffective against cancer, the disease affecting a large paying population. The African patients could not pay anything, so the drug companies could not profitably cover the fixed costs of bringing it back into production. In 2000, however, corporate interest in the precursor chemical to Eflornithine "soared because it might prevent the growth of facial hair in women."[8] Well-to-do American women would pay substantial sums for the drug, and the revenue from them alone would more than cover the fixed costs of bringing it back into production.[9] As a side benefit, the impoverished Africans could get access to the drug, but only because some paying customers shared their preference for this compound.

One might be tempted, at this point, to break into a story about evil drug companies. But that would be misguided for two reasons. First, in a market economy, private firms exist to make more money than they spend—and indeed have a responsibility to their shareholders to do just that. Second, the drug companies have, in a number of instances, helped poor victims of disease without hope of financial payoff.[10] Rather than a story about supposed malevolence in the pharmaceutical industry, this is a story about how markets function when products have substantial fixed costs.

The Eflornithine story vividly illustrates the "who benefits whom" phenomenon. When only poor Africans want Eflornithine, the revenue available to sellers cannot cover the fixed costs of bringing the drug into production. But when rich Western women share the poor Africans' preference for Eflornithine, the drug can be profitably brought to market. Who benefits whom? In this instance, wealthy, hirsute women benefit poor Africans by helping to make profitable a product they both desire.

While compelling, the Eflornithine story is merely an anecdote. I turn now to systematically documenting the phenomenon with data. While the operation of this phenomenon requires only two conditions—high fixed costs relative to market size, and preferences that differ across groups of consumers—systematically documenting the phenomenon requires additional conditions. First, I need multiple markets that differ in their mix of consumers, so we can see how that mix affects the mix of available products and, in turn, the satisfaction of various types of consumers. In particular, I need to see multiple markets, each of which is a self-contained unit of buyers and sellers. Second, documenting the phenomenon requires data on the numbers and characteristics of available products. Third, I need data on the tendency for different types of persons to consume products in the industry in question.

The geographic market is different for different products. Some goods, like restaurants, have very local neighborhood markets. Others, like local media firms, have metropolitan areas as their geographic markets. And goods that can be shipped great distances at low costs (considered in Part III) have global markets. What are some industries that meet the criteria for both the operation and detection of the "who benefits whom" phenomenon? At the metropolitan-area level, media markets, including radio, television, and newspapers, satisfy the conditions for both operation and detection. First, fixed costs are large enough so that markets accommodate few products. Second, as we will see, preferences in media content differ sharply across groups of consumers.

What about the conditions for detection? Can we observe multiple geographically distinct media markets? Although technology now makes it possible to make media content (audio, video, or text) available anywhere instantly, there are other limits on how far media content can be "shipped" without "spoilage." With the exception of the *New York Times,* with its extensive national and international coverage, local media content has little appeal outside of its home market. Hence, the market for daily newspapers remains almost entirely local. While newspapers are often not locally owned, they do provide an example of locally tailored supply serving local demand. Local editorial and production staffs produce local newspapers with both local and nonlocal content. While some stories are purchased from national wire services, the newspapers as a whole are tailored to local tastes and interests. Looking across U.S. metropolitan areas allows us to see how the local newspapers are tailored to local tastes and, in turn, which kinds of consumers benefit.

The same is true for conventional terrestrial radio. Radio stations require local physical facilities, and most radio stations have local on-air talent communicating messages and advertising to the local community. The products are pitched at only local demand, since broadcast signals are generally not available outside of the metropolitan areas where they originate.

Local television shares many of the features of radio and newspapers but differs in that much of what is aired on local stations originates elsewhere. Still, even local stations affiliated with national broadcast networks such as ABC, CBS, NBC, or Fox control many hours of programming per week. Local news programs, in particular, are not only locally controlled; they are also locally produced for local audiences.

Local media markets, then, give us an excellent empirical proving ground for documenting the "who benefits whom" and "tyranny of the majority" phenomena in product markets. Preferences for newspapers and radio programming differ sharply across groups of consumers. The industries provide examples of local supply serving local demand; in addition, because of advertisers' needs, data on available products and audience behavior are readily available, allowing us to observe multiple geographic markets differing in their mixes of consumers and products.

Radio Broadcasting

Commercial radio stations support themselves with advertising revenue. The more listeners they attract, and the more affluent the listeners, the more the station can charge for airing ads. Listeners pay for programming only indirectly by their willingness to listen to ads. Station owners face various costs, including the salaries of disc jockeys, engineers, and ad salespeople, as well as the capital costs for the broadcast facilities. All of the costs of creating and broadcasting radio programming are fixed costs because none vary with the number of listeners. Because of its fixed costs, a radio station in a medium-sized metropolitan area requires an average of about five thousand listeners, at any point in time, to break even. Roughly one-sixth of the population is listening at any point in time, so each station relies on an overall population of about thirty thousand.

Consequently, larger metropolitan areas have more radio stations. In 1997, Meridian, Mississippi (population 60,000) had two local radio stations, while New York City (population 14 million) had forty-four.[11] The relationship is quite consistent for cities in between. And larger markets not only offer more stations; they also present more programming variety. For example, in the late 1990s the Great Falls, Montana, area, population 65,400, had ten radio stations in six formats: four country stations, two "album-oriented rock" stations, and one each in oldies, Top 40, big band/nostalgia, and talk. Around the same time, the Minneapolis–St. Paul area—with a population of around three million—had twenty-three stations in eleven formats: eight in album-oriented rock, three each in big band/nostalgia and country, two in news/talk, and one each in adult contemporary, Top 40, full service, jazz, oldies, soft adult contemporary, and sports. The Philadelphia area, with nearly five million in population, had thirty stations in thirteen formats: including four each in black/urban, Top 40, and news/talk; three each in adult contemporary, oldies, and religion/gospel; two each in sports and big band/nostalgia; and one each in soft adult contemporary, jazz, classical, album-oriented rock, and country.

At one level it is no surprise that larger markets have more radio stations and more programming variety. What is surprising is not the statistical relationship per se but rather its meaning. According to the standard characterization of markets, each man can vote for the color of the tie he wants and get it. But surely there are some people among the 60,000 in Meridian or the 65,000 in Great Falls who would like to listen to classical music, jazz, or alternative rock. The market supplies these preference minorities with no such options. What they get depends not only on their own preferences, but also on the prevalence of those preferences in the market area.

If different people prefer different sorts of programming, then greater variety can allow more types of people to find appealing options. The usual approach that economists use to measure consumer satisfaction is to infer it from information about consumption and prices. That is, if someone purchases a product for, say, five dollars, she must value it at least as much as five dollars. Radio programming has the complicating feature that consumers get it for free. Those who choose to listen to radio prefer listening over silence, but since they pay no explicit price for programming, we cannot determine the dollar amount by which they prefer listening. Still, we can infer something about their satisfaction from their tendency to consume—that is, we can assume that the higher the tendency for members of a group to listen to radio, the greater their satisfaction. While crude, this method of tallying satisfaction is familiar from voting in political contexts. All persons pay essentially the same price to vote; hence their decision to vote does not indicate their intensity of preference for one candidate over the other, although it does reflect a desire to vote that was strong enough to get them to the polls.

Radio listening is higher in larger metropolitan areas, and this positive relationship holds after accounting for plausible determinants of radio listening such as commuting times.[12] In a larger metropolitan area, the larger potential audience allows broadcasters to attract enough listeners to cover the fixed costs of operating more stations.

Who Benefits Whom?

When there are fixed costs, people benefit from participating in markets with more consumers because additional consumers help bring forth more product options. But do all sorts of persons confer the same benefits on each other? If everyone liked the same sorts of music, then everyone would confer a similar benefit on each other. But as it turns out, preferences for radio programming differ sharply among people who differ in their race, Hispanic status, age, or gender.

The vast majority of radio stations in the United States broadcast programming in one of roughly forty discrete formats that seek to appeal to different groups of people. For example, Top 40 (or "contemporary hit radio") stations play music that appeals to listeners under age thirty, while "big-band/nostalgia" stations target persons over fifty. Some stations broadcast in Spanish, targeting Hispanic listeners, and other stations target black listeners. Perhaps not surprisingly, then, different formats attract very different groups of listeners. Because over-the-air broadcast signals are free, audience choices are not constrained by program prices or audience incomes. For this reason, information on radio and broadcast television use patterns provide unusually good data on preferences.

To analyze black and white preferences in radio programming, I assembled data on 1997 overall listening and black listening to each of the stations in one hundred metropolitan areas with large black populations, as well as 1997 overall and Hispanic listening to each of the stations in fifty-four metro areas with large Hispanic populations. These areas tend to have stations targeting blacks and Hispanics, respectively, so that listening patterns reflect choices among alternatives. The data are derived from Arbitron's spring 1997 audience surveys. Arbitron pays small sums of money to thousands of radio listeners for keeping diaries of their radio listening. I also have 1993 data on who listens to each of the stations in 163 metropolitan areas by age group and, separately, by gender. Industry data sources allow me to classify each of the stations into one of forty to fifty programming formats.

Table 1 shows how black and nonblack (for brevity, "white") listening is divided among the formats. The single most common programming format, and by far the most popular among whites, is country music. Country stations attract 12 percent of white listening but only 1.5 percent of black listening, so their audiences are disproportionately (over 97 percent) white.[13] Other formats attracting audiences over 95 percent white include album-oriented rock, classic album-oriented rock, and big band/nostalgia.

A few programming formats appeal to both blacks and whites. For example, jazz stations attract 6.5 percent of black listening and 2.3 percent of white listening, so that their audience is nearly 40 percent black. Top 40 stations that play black artists, labeled "urban contemporary hit radio" stations, as well as religious stations, as a group, also appeal to both blacks and whites.

TABLE 1 Radio listening preferences by group and format

	Percentage of group listening		Percentage of format listening that is Black
	Black	Non-black	
Narrowly black-targeted radio formats			
Black	32.5	1.7	81.7
Black/Adult Contemporary	18.3	0.8	84.8
Gospel	3.8	0.09	90.6
Black/Oldies	2.4	0.07	89.5
Black/Gospel	1.8	0.03	94.2
Black/Talk	1.4	0.03	91.3
Formats with black-white listening overlap			
Contemporary Hit Radio	7.7	2.7	40.2
Jazz	6.5	2.3	39.4
Religious	2.5	1.2	32.9
Other formats attracting substantial black listening			
Total	15.6	48.3	8.4
Formats appealing primarily to whites			
Country	1.5	11.9	3.1
Album-oriented Rock and Classic Album-oriented Rock	1.2	10.0	2.9
Big Band/Nostalgia	0.5	4.2	2.9

	Hispanic	Non-Hispanic	Percentage of format listening that is Hispanic
Narrowly Hispanic-targeted			
Spanish-language	45.7	0.5	96.2
Formats with Hispanic–non-Hispanic listening overlap			
Contemporary Hit Radio	8.6	6.0	29.5
Contemporary Hit Radio/Urban	6.4	4.2	30.5
Other formats attracting substantial Hispanic listening			
Total	34.0	72.7	12.0

Source: Adapted from Waldfogel (2003).

But the majority of black listening is concentrated in categories that attract few white listeners. Just over half of black listening is concentrated in only two formats, black, and black/adult contemporary, which account for less than 2.5 percent of "white" listening.[14] Altogether, black-targeted formats attract 60 percent of all black listeners, but only about 3 percent of white listeners. In short, blacks and whites tend to have very different preferences in radio programming.

How do black-targeted radio stations differ from their white-targeted counterparts? A major difference is the race of the artists and on-air personalities. The week I am writing this, according to *Radio & Records* magazine, the most played artists on black/adult contemporary (also called "urban/adult contemporary") are Alicia Keys, Brian McKnight, Anita Baker, Prince, Luther Vandross, Patti LaBelle, Ronald Isley, Jill Scott, Teena Marie, Gerald Levert, R. Kelly, and Kem. All of these artists but Teena Marie are African American.[15] The ten most played artists on "adult contemporary" radio for the same time period are Los Lonely Boys, Five for Fighting, Keith Urban, Maroon 5, Dido, Martina McBride, Kimberley Locke, Seal, Elton John, and Phil Collins, two of whom are black or include black members.[16] Black-targeted radio stations also tend to have black on-air personalities.[17]

Hispanics and non-Hispanics also have starkly different preferences in radio programming. The second part of Table 1 reports listening data, by format and Hispanic status, for the markets with Hispanic listening data. Hispanics make up an average of 25 percent of the population in the metropolitan areas with Hispanic listening data. Most formats, such as country, talk, news, as well as most black-targeted stations, attract audiences that are less than a quarter Hispanic. Two popular formats, Top 40 and urban Top 40, appeal to both Hispanic and non-Hispanic listeners, attracting audiences that are roughly a third Hispanic. Spanish-language radio attracts a disproportionately Hispanic audience: nearly half of Hispanic listeners (46 percent) choose Spanish-language radio. Like blacks and whites, then, Hispanics and non-Hispanics tend to have sharply different radio programming preferences.

Listeners of different ages also have dramatically different radio preferences.[18] For example, teenagers' listening is heavily concentrated in three formats, Top 40 (37.6 percent), black (19.3 percent), and album-oriented rock (11.5 percent), while radio listening of persons over age sixty-five is heavily concentrated in big band/nostalgia (14.0 percent), classical (3.6), full service (7.6), news and news/talk (16.3), and talk (14.0). Finally, preferences in radio differ somewhat between men and women. Album-oriented rock attracts 15 percent of male listening and only 7 percent of female listening, yielding an audience that is two-thirds male. Soft adult contemporary, by contrast, attracts 10 percent of women and only 6 percent of men, yielding an audience that is 60 percent female.

Although programming preferences differ substantially by age and somewhat by gender, the age and gender distributions of the population (for example, the share of population over age sixty-five) do not vary nearly as much across metropolitan areas as do the black or Hispanic shares. As a result, the "who benefits whom" and "tyranny of the majority" phenomena would be difficult to document along the dimensions of age and gender.

Different metropolitan areas do, however, have substantially different concentrations of black residents. Thus we can use the framework of Chapter 1 to think about the satisfaction that different sorts of people will derive from radio, given that preferences differ across ethnic and racial groups. Start with blacks and whites, and imagine a product spectrum running from black-targeted options at the far left to white-targeted options at the far right. In radio, the various "urban" formats would be at the far left, jazz and Top 40 would be in the middle, and country would be all the way to the right. In places with very few blacks, we would expect no black-targeted radio stations. In places with a sufficient black population, we would expect some black-targeted stations. In places with a large black population, we would expect more. Because blacks as a group tend to prefer black stations, we would thus expect blacks in areas with many black residents to be able to find radio stations nearer to their ideal station.

Of the 246 markets I studied, just over half have at least one local black-targeted radio station. And the tendency to have at least one such station increases not only with market size but also, and more particularly, with the number of blacks in the local area. Markets without any black-targeted stations average 13,000 blacks and 312,000 whites. Markets with one black station average 39,000 blacks and 513,000 whites.

Except for the fact that markets with fewer than about 15,000 blacks have no black-targeted stations, the relationship between the fraction black in a metropolitan area and the share of stations targeting black listeners is roughly proportional. In metropolitan areas that are 10 percent black, roughly 8 percent of radio stations are black-targeted. As the fraction of population that is black increases, the share of radio stations targeting blacks increases as well. The same relationships hold for Spanish-language (and other Hispanic-targeted programming) and the local Hispanic population. Thus the mix of available radio stations is highly sensitive to the mix of potential listeners in the area. In places with more blacks, blacks are likely to find more options that appeal to them. Likewise for Hispanics.

How about direct evidence on satisfaction? When we examine listening by race, we see that not all groups confer similar benefits on each other. Consider the respective relationships between the black and white tendencies to listen to the radio and local black and white (nonblack) populations. Black listening increases sharply with black population, while black listening does not vary with white population. An additional million whites in a metropolitan area raises white listening by about 0.4 percentage points on a base of 13 percent, or by about 3 percent. An additional million blacks raises black listening by 2.7 percentage points on a base of 18 percent, or by about 15 percent. For black listening, the difference between being in a metropolitan area at the ninetieth percentile of black population (0.5 million blacks) and the tenth percentile (30,000 blacks) is 1.25 percentage points of the population listening, or nearly a tenth of the average black listening rate.[19] That is, in their capacity as radio listeners, blacks benefit from having other blacks in their market areas, but they do not benefit from having additional whites.

Analogously, white listening bears a positive relationship to white population but no relationship to black population. In short, as radio listeners, whites benefit from the presence of other whites in the market, but they do not benefit from having additional blacks in the market.

These are striking results. Larger markets bring forth more products, which might in principle offer greater satisfaction to all consumers. But the mix of products is sensitive to the mix of consumers, and because blacks and whites prefer different products, they benefit themselves and not each other in this product market. Similar patterns hold for Hispanics and non-Hispanics.

These results provide clear evidence of the "who benefits whom" phenomenon. When fixed costs are large and preferences differ across consumers, then when allocation occurs through markets, people get what they want only if others are also prepared to pay for it. As a result, consumers benefit from participating in a product market with others who share their preferences. We saw this in pharmaceutical products, and we see it in radio as well. This evidence shows the radio market to be a far cry from hypothetical neckties, available to an individual because he alone wants one.

Daily Newspapers

We saw in the radio example how a differentiated product market functions with fixed costs that are substantial enough to limit the industry to an average of twenty products per metropolitan area. Newspaper markets offer even fewer products per metropolitan area: a typical metropolitan area in the United States has one daily paper, and its publisher has to decide how to pitch it to a somewhat—or very—diverse population. In so doing, she may be able to please one group but not another.

The notion that one group's growth could actually hurt another group of product consumers may sound implausible. Yet daily newspapers' recent efforts to target Hispanic readers provide an interesting case study. Hispanics are not only a substantial share of U.S. population; they are also the fastest growing major group. The Hispanic population grew from less than 5 percent of the U.S. population in 1970, to nearly 10 percent in 1990, to 12.5 percent in 2000.[20] Hispanics and Anglos differ in their newspaper preferences. First, many Hispanics prefer newspapers in Spanish rather than English. Second, many topics, such as Latin American affairs and soccer, command greater interest among the Latin community. And third, according to some experts, Latin readers prefer to see splashy newspaper graphics as well as opinion on the front page.[21]

Newspaper circulation has declined steadily in the United States since the diffusion of television.[22] Newspaper publishers view the growth opportunity of burgeoning Hispanic populations as a way to stem the decline. But attracting Hispanic readers without alienating Anglos is difficult.

The experience of the newspaper in Racine, Wisconsin, illustrates the inherent challenge of trying to appeal to multiple groups with a single product. The *Journal-Times,* facing a growing Hispanic population in Racine, tried to reposition itself to appeal to the potential new readers. They incorporated a full page of Spanish language news, summarized in English. But according to *Editor and Publisher* magazine in 2004: "In the fraying-blue-collar town with a high unemployment rate and an inchoate resentment of illegal immigrants, the sudden transformation of the 'A' section's second page from English to Spanish unnerved—even unhinged—some longtime readers when it first appeared." According to editor Randolph Brandt, "We anticipated some complaints. What we didn't anticipate was that the reaction would be so vociferous." Moreover, "Scores of readers threatened to cancel their subscriptions. A couple of dozen actually did, and it began to look like the cancellations would continue every time the page ran. Not only was the test failing to expand readership, it jeopardized the rest of the paper."[23]

The Racine experience is not isolated. According to the same source, "Utah's third-biggest daily, the *Standard-Examiner* in Ogden, tried a bilingual page a few years ago that failed in part because of resentment by English-language readers."[24]

Nowhere is the growth in Hispanics more pronounced than Miami, where the Hispanic population has grown from 5 percent in 1960 to 65 percent in 2000. One observer remarked that in "the 1970's, Miami was a Jewish retirement community. This is the exact same place that was little brown Jewish women laying in the sun. Today it is Hispanic women on Roller Blades."[25]

How has the rapid change in the composition of Miami's population played out through the newspaper market? As Miami's Hispanic population grew, the *Miami Herald*, the area's only major daily paper, sought to woo Hispanic readers. Their first foray was a "couple of pages" in Spanish. It later grew to a newspaper-within-a-newspaper called *el Miami Herald* and later *el Nuevo Herald*. But the paper remained hidden inside the fat *Miami Herald*, "a pound of English covering a quarter-pound of Spanish," according to its publisher. This "double-duty" product met with mixed success among Hispanic readers. According to its publisher, the "customer was taking the Spanish-language paper out of the Herald, putting the English-language paper back and leaving a quarter on the counter—at a time when the *Herald* cost thirty-five cents. The store owner pockets the quarter and we give him credit for an unsold paper." Added the publisher, the "market had spoken in favor of a separate paper."[26]

These stories about wooing Hispanic readers suggest that additional Hispanics in a metropolitan area make non-Hispanic readers worse off as newspaper consumers, and vice versa. In short, they suggest that the tyranny of the majority operates in this product market. Are the anecdotes borne out by more systematic analysis of the daily newspaper industry?

While perhaps not as extreme as the linguistic differences that distinguish Hispanic and non-Hispanic readers, blacks and whites, as groups, also prefer different kinds of newspapers. This is clear from their different product choices in the metropolitan areas with multiple newspapers. For example, there are two major contrasting newspapers available in Chicago, Boston, and Philadelphia. Each city has a broadsheet and a tabloid. The tabloid layout has traditionally appealed to commuters using public transit because its pages are easier to turn in a crowded space. The tabloids also cover the news differently.

The broadsheets devote more coverage to "hard news" (national, international, and business news), while the tabloids focus more on "soft news" (such as entertainment and sports reporting). How do black and white customers respond? Within each of these metropolitan areas, the tabloid's market share is much higher in heavily black neighborhoods. The higher the fraction black in a zip code, the higher the market share of the tabloid relative to the broadsheet.[27] As a result, the implied broadsheet market share in a heavily black zip code (at the ninety-fifth percentile of black population shares, which is 48 percent black) is twenty percentage points lower than in a predominantly white one (at the fifth percentile by black population shares, which is almost all white). It seems that black consumers, as a group, typically prefer the tabloids.[28]

While not as stark as a preference for reading in English rather than in Spanish, the different preferences among blacks and whites still suggest that newspapers can target one group only at the expense of another.

Newspaper Targeting

There are far fewer daily newspapers than radio stations per area. Indeed, product differentiation in daily newspapers takes a very different form than in radio stations. Rather than forty to fifty different discrete programming formats, daily newspapers generally differ in three ways: length, writing style, and topical coverage (for example, local versus national, hard news versus soft). In choosing their approach for these three variables—whether they consciously seek to or not—newspapers can appeal more or less to black readers.

As we would expect if papers are trying to attract readers from the local community, paper targeting differs across markets with the share of the potential consumers who are black. This is evident from the relationship between reporters in hard news and the black population share in the metropolitan area: the share of reporters in soft news is higher in markets with a larger black share. How substantial is the relationship? Compared with an all-white metropolitan area, an area that is 50 percent black would have 50 percent, as opposed to 60 percent, of its reporters and editors allocated to hard news.[29]

In markets with more blacks, the newspaper(s) in town position themselves nearer to black consumers' preferences. How does this affect the tendency for various types of persons to purchase a newspaper? Are whites more likely to purchase a local paper in a market where the paper targets white preferences? Are blacks more likely to purchase a paper in a metropolitan area with a more heavily black population? Do more blacks in a market make whites less likely to buy the paper, and vice versa?

Answering these questions requires a bit of ingenuity given the sorts of data systematically available. I do not observe the tendency for individuals to purchase newspapers, but I have been able to analyze the circulation of local daily newspapers, as well as demographic characteristics, by zip code. These data have allowed me to document the relationship between black and white metropolitan area populations and the tendencies for the respective groups to purchase the newspaper using an indirect approach.

First, the higher the share of a zip code's population that is black, the lower the per capita newspaper circulation in the zip code. This reflects a black-white reading gap, or a depressed tendency for blacks to buy newspapers, relative to whites (for a variety of historical and economic reasons). The "who benefits whom" question is reflected in the way the white-black newspaper gap varies across metropolitan areas with their respective black and white populations. If papers more closely target black preferences in heavily black metropolitan areas, then in such areas, the local paper should be relatively more appealing to blacks, and the gap between black and white reading will be smaller. By contrast, in metro areas where the white population is larger and black population smaller, the local newspaper will be correspondingly more appealing to whites and less appealing to blacks—and the black-white circulation gap will be larger.

This is precisely what happens. As in radio, the tendency of blacks to buy the local paper is very sensitive to the size of the local black population. An additional million blacks in the metropolitan area raise the black tendency to read the newspaper by about 0.15 copies per capita. The average per capita circulation rate for blacks and whites together is 0.21, and the circulation rate in heavily black zip codes is lower. Hence, an additional million blacks raises the black circulation rate by over 75 percent. An additional million whites raises the white tendency to read the paper much less, by about 0.01 (or about 5 percent of the average per capita circulation rate). Why do blacks benefit blacks more than whites benefit whites? Because whites vastly outnumber blacks almost everywhere. There are enough whites everywhere to ensure that publishers target products in ways that appeal to whites. Black metropolitan area populations, by contrast, are in many areas tiny. Going from a large white population to a huge one does not make the paper substantially more appealing to whites. But shifting from a tiny black population to, say, a quarter of the population will tend to bring about a more substantial improvement in the product from the perspective of blacks.

Not only are within-group effects positive; cross-group effects are negative in one direction (running from whites to blacks) and zero in the other. That is, additional whites reduce the tendency for blacks to purchase the paper, while additional blacks have no effect on the white tendency to purchase the paper. An additional million whites reduce per capita black circulation by 0.03, or by over 15 percent. This effect provides large-scale statistical evidence of the tyranny of the majority in a product market.

In daily newspaper markets, as in radio markets, we see the "who benefits whom" phenomenon clearly: blacks benefit blacks, and whites benefit whites in their respective capacities as newspaper consumers. But the workings of the even-higher-fixed-cost newspaper market go beyond this phenomenon. Like radio markets, newspaper markets lack the "go home happy" feature of perfectly competitive markets. First, in contrast to Friedman's hypothetical ties, I don't get the sort of newspaper that I want just because I want it. I get what I want if many other people also want it. Second, a larger population preferring something else actually makes me worse off, thereby failing to avoid strains on social cohesion. This evidence stands in stark contrast with many idealized portraits of markets.

The radio and newspaper examples illustrate the benefits that consumers derive from having others who share their preferences in the same market. But the meaning of "being in the same market" varies greatly across different industries. For local newspaper and radio, the relevant geographic area is the metropolitan area. In their capacity as newspaper readers and radio listeners, blacks and Hispanics benefit from living in the same metropolitan area as other blacks and Hispanics. For goods such as pharmaceutical products that are traded nationally or globally, by contrast, where availability depends on the revenue available from potential buyers in the nation or the world, there is no benefit of locating in a particular place for having access to the product. Sub-Saharan Africans suffering from sleeping sickness can benefit from beauty-conscious American women. Other examples include automobiles, which are routinely produced in Asia for sale in Europe or North America. The clothing market, too, is very global. Visit an Old Navy store in the United States and you will see clothing made in countries on almost every continent.

At the other extreme are products that transport only short distances, such as restaurant food or religious services. As we shall see in Chapter 4, their availability depends on the mix of consumers who are very nearby.

Who Benefits Whom
in the Neighborhood

On Saturday mornings, when I'm driving my daughters to and from their basketball games in Lower Merion township, a close suburb of Philadelphia, I frequently pass groups of pedestrians walking and pushing strollers. The men wear dark clothing and long coats. The women wear long skirts and headscarves. The eastern end of the township is densely populated with Orthodox Jews. Why do Orthodox Jewish people cluster in this neighborhood? What benefit do they derive from living near others who share their preferences in food, styles of worship, and other aspects of life? Although the public schools, parks, and other services may be a draw, they are excellent throughout the township, so this cannot explain the neighborhood clustering of Orthodox Jews. Rather, the answer lies in the interaction between Jewish law and the economics of product differentiation with fixed costs.

First, Orthodox Jewish religious services are a differentiated product. Reform or conservative services, conducted in English and with direct participation by women, are an unacceptable alternative to Orthodox services for many Orthodox Jews. Second, the production of Jewish services entails fixed costs, in that Jewish law requires a minyan of ten men to conduct a religious service. In order to produce an Orthodox service, one must therefore coordinate with at least nine other Orthodox men. A synagogue's "catchment area" must include enough Orthodox Jewish men so that at least ten will always be in attendance for services.

Finally, Orthodox Jews are not allowed to drive during the Sabbath. As a result, observant Orthodox Jews must live within walking distance of their temple. In this instance, the market for religious services gives rise to the clustering of at least ten male Orthodox Jews within walking distance of each synagogue.

This example provides a metaphor for the benefits that consumers, especially those with atypical product preferences, can derive from living in the same neighborhood with others who share their preferences. Using the restaurant market as its context, this chapter provides systematic empirical evidence about product market benefits of highly local residential clustering of like-minded consumers. That is, here I revisit the question of who benefits whom for products with small, neighborhood-level geographic markets.

Chapter 3 provided clear evidence that groups affect each other through local media markets at the metropolitan-area level and, moreover, that different groups affect each other differently. Additional blacks bring forth more black-targeted local media products and tend to increase blacks' consumption and satisfaction. Similarly, additional whites and Hispanics benefit whites and Hispanics, respectively, in local media markets. Given their sharply different preferences, blacks and whites do not benefit each other in local media markets; and in the daily newspaper market, they can actually harm each other. But are these documented effects peculiar to markets with very high fixed costs, such as local media markets and pharmaceuticals? Or do these phenomena also arise in other sorts of markets?

If the "who benefits whom" phenomenon is widespread, we should be able to document product-market effects of one group on another in different sorts of industries, including those with much smaller fixed costs than local media firms. But which industries should one examine? Empirical social scientists need to be opportunistic, drawing lessons from industries for which data are systematically available. Restaurants are an example of a low fixed cost industry for which data are readily available. Many restaurants are part of chains, which makes their targeting easy to classify. And because restaurants sell directly to the general public, their locations are not only public information but also easy to obtain, for example from phone directories.

Under two simple conditions, the restaurant market will provide a mechanism for clusters of like-minded people to benefit each other as food consumers. First, food preferences must differ substantially between groups. Second, the fixed costs of operating restaurants must be large enough that restaurants appealing to each group only arise with sufficient local concentrations of persons favoring a particular variety. Under those conditions, neighborhoods with more members of a particular group will be more likely to have restaurants catering to the group's preferences.

While it is plausible that food preferences differ by group, it is less obvious that the second condition holds for restaurants. First, restaurants' fixed costs are simply not very large. In the other industries we have examined so far, fixed costs are quite large relative to market size. The number of products per market provides a rough (implicit) measure of fixed costs in relation to market size. Metropolitan areas average twenty radio stations, five to seven broadcast television stations, and no more than a handful of daily newspapers. Restaurants are plentiful in comparison. A metro area of one million persons has about 1,500 restaurants, and there are half a million restaurants in the United States, approximately one for every six hundred persons. The fixed cost of operating a restaurant is of a lower order of magnitude than that for local media firms. Thus, on the one hand, the restaurant market appears to have a densely packed product space, with products at every conceivable point on the spectrum and therefore no consumers without local product options near their ideal. It does not appear that a consumer needs many like-minded preference confederates to make his desired restaurant profitable.

On the other hand, a restaurant's geographic market is potentially much smaller than the global markets for drugs or perhaps even local media products. If so, then even a large number of restaurants per metropolitan area would not guarantee small fixed costs in comparison with the relevant market. For example, if people only travel short distances to restaurants, then the number of effective options may include only restaurants in a few-mile radius rather than an entire metropolitan area. And if preferences differ across groups of consumers, small groups with distinct preferences may have access to few, or no, appealing options.[1] So who benefits whom in the neighborhood?[2]

What is the Relevant Geographic Market?

How big is the geographic market for a restaurant, and how does it compare with the market area for local media products? Except when they are traveling, consumers only patronize restaurants within their metropolitan areas. Different types of restaurants have different-sized market areas, however. A four-star downtown restaurant patronized on special occasions draws customers from throughout the metropolitan area. Fast food restaurants, however, have smaller market areas. For example, the Louisville, Kentucky, metropolitan area, with a population of about one million, has 59 McDonald's, 33 KFCs, 32 Taco Bells, 2 TGI Friday's, and 6 Bob Evanses. Restaurant firms do not want their outlets to compete with each other, so the existence of multiple locations within a metropolitan area is, on its face, evidence that their geographic markets are much smaller than the metropolitan area.

Data on the number of restaurants by place allow more systematic inferences about the size of the market area for restaurants. If the demand for restaurants arose from within geographic areas, then we would expect a strong relationship between geographic area demand (measured, say, by population) and the number of restaurants operating. Indeed, a relationship between restaurants and population at some level of geographic aggregation indicates that supply for that area serves demand at—or within—that level of geography. Data on population and the number of restaurants in each zip code provide clues about the effective size of restaurants' geographic markets.[3] A three-digit zip code includes all five-digit zip codes that begin with the same first three digits. Three-digit zip codes average about a thousand square miles of overall land and water area. If they were circular, they would have an average radius of 15.1 miles.[4] Given their size—and given how far people typically travel to restaurants—it is safe to assume that restaurants in a three-digit zip code draw their customers from within the area.

There is a strong positive relationship between population and restaurants at the three-digit zip code level, and this relationship indicates that restaurants draw their patrons from their respective areas (or, at least, that "exports" and "imports" balance). A three-digit zip code with an additional one thousand persons has 1.51 more restaurants.

Three-digit zip code areas are large, and people within metropolitan areas do not generally travel fifteen miles for a restaurant meal. Is there a similarly strong relationship between population and restaurants—between demand and supply—in smaller geographic areas? If so, that would indicate that supply serves demand for smaller areas, or that the relevant geographic market for restaurants is smaller than a three-digit zip code. Five-digit zip codes are far smaller than three-digit zip code areas; they average forty-seven square miles, with a (hypothetically circular) mean radius of three miles. It turns out that among five-digit zip codes, too, there is a clear positive relationship between population and the number of restaurants operating, indicating that even at this finer level of geography, restaurants locate where the customers are.

Regardless of the level of geography analyzed, an additional one thousand persons raises the number of restaurants in the area by between 1.4 and 1.6. This observation has two implications. First, the geographic market for most restaurants is small. While it is surely true that consumers sometimes travel outside their zip codes to obtain restaurant food, it appears that the extent to which consumers from one zip code travel to restaurants in another zip code is balanced by travel in the opposite direction. In that sense, restaurant "exports" balance "imports" across zip codes. And the five-digit zip codes provide a reasonable approximation of the market area for restaurants. The practical implication of this finding is that we can treat the five-digit zip code as the relevant market area for restaurants.

Second, as with radio stations in a metropolitan area, more potential customers bring forth more products. We can think of restaurants as differentiated by both location and cuisine. Having more restaurants means, in general, having more persons who will find restaurants that suit their tastes. If all sorts of people liked a similar mix of restaurants, then all people would exert similar beneficial effects on each other through product markets. But preferences differ.

Do Restaurant Preferences Differ by Group?

Introspection and casual experience suggest that different groups patronize different restaurants. Systematic data confirm this. A 1999–2000 survey of 180,000 conducted by Scarborough Research asked people differing by race, Hispanic status, and education which of a long list of chain restaurants they had patronized in the past thirty days. The chains include fifty-nine fast food and seventy-seven sit-down restaurants. These data cover most of the top fifty chains, which generated $96.4 billion in 2002 revenue, or about 20 percent of total U.S. restaurant industry revenue.[5]

The restaurants also vary systematically in their fare, both by cuisine and price. The chains include both fast food and sit-down restaurants, and their menus (which I generally found at their websites), allow their classification into six groups: chicken (including Chick-fil-A, Church's Fried Chicken, KFC, Popeye's Chicken and Biscuits), pizza (such as Domino's, Pizza Hut, Papa John's, Little Caesars, and Bertucci's), hamburger (McDonald's, Burger King, Wendy's, Checkers, and so on), Mexican (including Taco Bell, Taco Time, and El Pollo Loco), steak (including Golden Corral, Lonestar, Outback, Ruth's Chris), and coffee/bagel (like Starbucks, Dunkin' Donuts, Einstein Bros. Bagels, Noah's Bagels), as well as a not-elsewhere-classified group. Consumer Reports' annual restaurant survey data allow us to classify fifty-two of these chains by price range for a typical check, reflecting the "average amount readers paid for their own dinner and drinks, excluding tip": under ten dollars (such as Denny's or International House of Pancakes), eleven to fourteen dollars (such as Applebee's or Ruby Tuesday), fifteen to nineteen dollars (such as Bertucci's or Olive Garden), twenty to twenty-four dollars (for example, Houston), twenty-five to twenty-nine dollars (none in our sample), and over thirty-five dollars (Ruth's Chris).[6]

Classifying the data this way, we see that blacks and whites systematically patronize different restaurants. (Significantly, this argument does not require preferences to differ because of race. Rather, I am simply classifying people into "blacks" and "whites" as two groups with different preferences.) As we see in Table 2, blacks are far more likely to patronize chicken chains than whites. Similarly, blacks are somewhat more likely than whites to patronize Long John Silver's and Red Lobster.[7] On the basis of the evidence in Table 2, these blacks and whites appear to have different preferences in prepared food.

The difference between black and white food preferences is not surprising in light of historical accounts of the development of Afri-

TABLE 2 Who patronizes which chain restaurants? (percentages)

	White	Black	Non-Hispanic	Hispanic	No College	College
Fast food chains, by type						
Burger	25.9	34.5	26.8	30.6	28.4	24.3
Chicken	11.2	22.6	12.9	15.1	13.6	12.0
Coffee/bagel	7.4	6.8	7.2	6.4	5.4	10.6
Mexican	22.0	23.5	21.0	28.5	7.5	8.5
Pizza	10.2	11.8	9.2	15.0	10.4	9.4
Sit-down chains, by price range						
Under $10	10.2	13.5	10.5	12.2	11.1	9.6
$10–$15	8.6	8.3	8.6	9.2	7.8	10.1
Over $15	7.0	7.6	7.2	7.0	6.3	8.6

Source: Calculated from Scarborough Research data described in Waldfogel (2006).
Note: The table shows the percentage of the various groups patronizing various sorts of chain restaurants within the last thirty days. A person can patronize more than one type of restaurant, so totals can exceed 100.

can American cuisine. According to one account, "With an array of new ingredients at their fingertips and a well-tuned African palate, the cooks would make delectable foods for their masters. Suddenly southern cooking took on new meaning. Fried chicken began to appear on the tables, sweet potatoes (which had replaced the African yam) sat next to the boiled white potato."[8]

The cuisines mentioned in these accounts fall under the categories of "southern cuisine," as well as Creole and Cajun. Particular foods include fried chicken, various shrimp recipes, catfish, hush puppies, crab cakes, cornbread muffins, and buttermilk biscuits.

Some of these foods feature prominently in the offerings of chain restaurants. In particular, fried chicken is the featured offering of four major chains in our sample: KFC, Church's Fried Chicken, Bojangle's, and Popeye's Chicken and Biscuits. Seafood is the featured food at Long John Silver's and Red Lobster. On the basis of the historical accounts, it is not surprising that these restaurants are disproportionately patronized by black consumers.

Do restaurant preferences differ by Hispanic status? While the term "Hispanic" covers a broad range of national backgrounds, nearly 60 percent of Hispanics in the United States are of Mexican extraction.[9] Perhaps Mexican restaurants cater to Hispanic tastes, but casual observation suggests that non-Hispanic consumers are major patrons of Mexican restaurants.

Table 2 shows that the Hispanic tendency to patronize listed Mexican restaurants is higher than the non-Hispanic tendency. While nearly 30 percent of Hispanics have visited a Mexican restaurant in the past thirty days, just over 20 percent of non-Hispanics had. Hispanics also are more likely to visit a number of burger and pizza restaurants. The results in Table 2 suggest that, in general, Hispanic and non-Hispanic preferences differ somewhat, although less than the differences between black and white restaurant preferences.

Do restaurant preferences differ by income? The Scarborough data report income only for a subset but education for the entire sample. Given the strong relationship between income and education, we examine restaurant patronage by whether people have completed college. Three things emerge from examination of Table 2. First, college-educated persons patronize coffee and bagel restaurants far more than their less-educated counterparts (roughly double for Bruegger's Bagels, Einstein Bros. Bagels, Noah's Bagels, and Starbucks Coffee). Second, those who are college educated are also less likely to patronize chicken restaurants. Third, college-educated persons are more likely to patronize more expensive sit-down restaurants among the sit-down establishments that Consumer Reports classifies by price range.[10] College-educated persons are more likely than their less-educated counterparts to patronize sit-down chains with higher prices. By contrast, the college-educated are relatively less likely to patronize low-priced sit-down chain restaurants.

It is clear that restaurant preferences differ across groups, particularly by race and by education/income. In addition, because customers do not travel far to patronize restaurants, fixed costs may be large relative to the relevant market. Do neighborhoods with like-minded consumers, then, attract restaurants that suit local tastes and, moreover, do consumers derive greater satisfaction from restaurants when they are surrounded by like-minded consumers?

If You Come, Will They Build It?

Places with more people have more restaurants. Zip codes with 5–10,000 people have a mean (median) of 11 (9) restaurants, while zip codes with 20,000–25,000 people have an average of 40 (35). In this sense, as for other products, people benefit each other generally by helping to bring forth more products. But do all sorts of people bring forth additional restaurants to a similar extent? Zip codes differ both in demographic mix as well as overall population, and this variation gives rise to variation in the mix of local restaurants. The 15,000 zip codes that correspond to U.S. metropolitan areas vary enormously in their composition by race, ethnicity, and college attainment—all factors related to product preferences. The median zip code by race is 2.1 percent black, the median by Hispanic status is 2.7 percent Hispanic, and the median by share educated is 15.9 percent college educated. The ninetieth-percentile zip codes, meanwhile, are nearly a third black, Hispanic, and college educated, respectively.

Looking across the 15,000 metro area zip codes, we see that the more blacks, Hispanics, or non–college graduates there are nearby, holding total population constant, the fewer overall restaurants operate nearby. This is not surprising, given that blacks, Hispanics, and those who have not attended college tend to have less money than whites, non-Hispanics, and the college educated. But what about the restaurants that particularly target blacks, Hispanics, or college-educated persons?[11]

To answer this question, I consulted Yellow Pages data (from the Reference USA directory) on the number of outlets in each of the

TABLE 3 What's available in a five-digit zip code?

	All	Areas over 50% black	Areas over 50% Hispanic	Areas over 36% college-educated
Restaurants overall	88.0	91.6	74.4	82.2
Fast food chains	63.3	77.8	61.2	60.5
Sit-down chains	40.6	38.1	41.5	39.9
Burger	52.9	66.0	55.9	42.1
Chicken	31.1	59.1	38.9	21.7
Coffee/Bagel	27.5	20.2	21.0	51.6
Mexican	26.1	23.1	30.3	17.6
Pizza	41.7	40.6	43.2	38.4
Steak	10.8	6.5	4.5	17.6
By price range				
Under $10	23.9	16.9	23.2	17.7
$10–15	16.7	9.2	10.1	18.9
Over $15	13.2	8.8	6.5	20.0
N	14,954	811	796	978

Note: The table shows the percentage of zip codes containing various kinds of restaurants. The calculations include only metropolitan-area five-digit zip codes. Five-digit zip codes average fifty square miles in a combination of land and water which, if it were circular, implies a radius of three miles.

Source: Derived from calculations in Waldfogel (2006).

136 restaurant chains, by zip code. This comes to 300,000 restaurants, of the half a million total U.S. restaurants in 2000.

How many restaurants of each type are available in each five-digit zip code? As Table 3 shows, almost 90 percent of the five-digit zip codes have at least one restaurant, and nearly two-thirds have at least one of our chain restaurants. The presence of sample chains serving different cuisines varies substantially. Hamburgers are the most widely available chain cuisine: over half of the five-digit zip codes have at least one of the hamburger chains. Pizza is next, available through one of the chains in 42 percent of five-digit zip codes. Just over 31 percent of five-digit zip codes have one of the chicken chains, 28 percent have coffee/bagel chains, and 26 percent have a sample Mexican chain. Steak chains are far less prevalent; 10.8 percent of zip codes have a sample steak chain.

Nearly a quarter of the zip codes have at least one location of one of the chains charging under ten dollars for a meal. The more expensive sample chains are less prevalent: chains charging ten to fifteen dollars are present in 17 percent of zip codes, and the sample chains charging over fifteen dollars are present in only 13 percent of zip codes.

Do people tend to find more restaurants that appeal to them when more of their neighbors share their preferences? For example, are blacks more likely to find southern cuisine in heavily black neighborhoods? Heavily black zip codes are slightly more likely than average zip codes to have a fast-food restaurant among sample chains and slightly less likely to have a sample sit-down chain. But two contrasts stand out in Table 3, which shows the availability of various types of restaurants in the five-digit zip codes that are most heavily black, Hispanic, and college-educated. First, heavily black zip codes are substantially more likely than metropolitan zip codes overall to have at least one sample chicken chain: nearly 60 percent of heavily black zip codes, as opposed to 30 percent of overall zip codes, have a sample chicken chain. Second, heavily college-educated zip codes are substantially more likely than zip codes overall, at 52 versus 27 percent, to have a coffee/bagel restaurant.

The presence of high- and low-priced restaurants is also sensitive to the composition of a zip code's population. The more expensive chains are less prevalent than the least expensive sit-down chains, and the pattern is pronounced for the predominantly black and Hispanic zip codes. The pattern is reversed, however, for the high-income zip codes where over 36 percent of the adult population is college educated. More expensive restaurants are more prevalent where more people have more to spend.

The restaurant patronage data indicate that sample coffee/bagel chains, as well as expensive restaurants, appeal to educated persons and that sample chicken chains appeal to black consumers. Hence the elevated presence of these respective chain types in heavily educated and black areas provides confirming evidence of the who-benefits-whom phenomenon in the restaurant market: people find more appealing options in product markets if their market area contains a heavier concentration of persons sharing their preferences.

Lacking information on consumption, I instead draw inferences about consumers' satisfaction from their proximity to appealing restaurants. So, what do the data show? Recall that five-digit zip codes would average six miles in diameter if they were circular. Residents of 30 percent of metropolitan area zip codes have a sample chicken chain within about three miles (the radius of a zip code). People in six-tenths of the 811 zip codes that are most heavily black have a sample chicken chain within about three miles. One can tell a similar story about proximity to coffee/bagel restaurants in heavily educated zip codes versus zip codes overall.[12]

The "findings" that fried chicken chains locate in black neighborhoods, while Starbucks and Einstein Bros. Bagels locate in higher-income neighborhoods, will surprise few people who have traveled about in major U.S. cities. What's novel here is not the fact but rather its interpretation. A typical neighborhood has a limited number of restaurant options and therefore does not have choices that appeal to every person. A consumer does not get whatever option he wants, even in a low fixed cost industry like restaurants. Instead, he gets what he wants if his neighborhood has enough people who share his preferences.

Until this point we have been implicitly talking about an effect of population mix on product mix. And, indeed, it is natural to suppose that sellers tailor their offerings to local consumers. But individuals also choose where to live, in part based on the mix of products available locally. Thus one implication of the "who benefits whom" phenomenon is that people can benefit from participating in markets with others sharing their preferences. For products that are easily transported, one can benefit from distant consumers sharing one's preferences. For products that are local in nature, however, such as restaurant food, religious services, or most retailing, one needs to live in a concentration of persons sharing one's preferences to benefit from them. For local media products, deriving benefits simply requires choosing a metropolitan area with a sufficient concentration of preference compatriots.[13] For restaurants, by contrast, it requires choosing a neighborhood with a sufficient concentration.

Individuals can respond to—and protect themselves from—the "who benefits whom" phenomenon by choosing where to live. Indeed, the persistence of racial segregation even as explicit racial barriers have eroded may stem in part from the desire of blacks for access to products that only agglomeration allows (a point that is not meant to overlook the serious problems of poverty and remaining tacit segregation).[14] In addition to restaurants, it is easy to imagine retail more generally, as well as churches, as high-fixed-cost differentiated products that individuals might cluster together to jointly consume.

The relationship between neighborhood clusters of people and products targeting them contains both good and bad news for preference minorities. The bad news is that the "who benefits whom" phenomenon arises in a wider range of markets than would have been obvious. The good news, however, is that people can improve their access to products with narrow appeal by choosing to live in a neighborhood with like-minded consumers. One could, in principle, choose which city to live in this way. Choosing a neighborhood is even easier.

It is customary to think of people choosing their communities on the basis of some products, in particular public schools and parks. The process of individuals sorting into communities that match their preferences for schooling expenditure and taxes is thought to be the way that local government-provided goods can be allocated efficiently.[15] As this chapter shows, however, residential sorting has private-product market implications as well.

Taken together, the results on media industries and restaurants provide a wealth of evidence for the central point: when fixed costs are large relative to market size, consumers get what they want from differentiated product markets only to the extent that others want similar things. The usually assumed dichotomy between markets and voting is clearly violated in these circumstances. Markets do not allow consumers to get whatever they want just because they alone want it; instead, in a variety of industrial contexts, markets share the fractious features of allocation through politics.

CHAPTER 5

Preference Minorities
as Citizens and Consumers

To this point we have seen that the consequence of a product's availability is that consumers purchase it and experience satisfaction. But consumer satisfaction is not the only possible effect of product availability. Media products offer both entertainment and information, and entertainment consumption is an end in itself. Information is different. Generally, people do not watch the Weather Channel because they enjoy it; they watch it to find out how to dress their children in the morning or whether they should carry an umbrella to work. Similarly, most people do not read, watch, or listen to the news primarily for entertainment. Rather, they do so to get information on how to conduct their lives, including whether and how to vote.

Universal suffrage in the United States has been attained slowly over time. The framers of the Constitution could not agree on who could vote, leaving it to individual states to decide. Many imposed property ownership requirements, and the last state to abandon the property requirement was North Carolina in 1856. While the Fifteenth Amendment to the U.S. Constitution gave black males the right to vote in 1870, many states imposed poll taxes or other requirements to prevent blacks from voting. With the Nineteenth Amendment in 1920, women won the right to vote. And states' uses of poll taxes and other schemes to prevent blacks from voting were barred by the Twenty-fourth Amendment in 1964.[1]

Today, whether people vote depends less on formal or informal restrictions and more on the information they possess, in particular, information communicated through media products like those discussed in Chapter 3. There we saw that preference minorities, small groups with locally atypical preferences, faced less or less appealing programming in local media products. Only places with large concentrations of black or Hispanic residents can support black- or Hispanic-targeted media outlets. If group-targeted information sources make it easier for targeted individuals to be informed about civic matters, then the "who benefits whom" phenomenon may affect whether people vote, as well as what they can consume. That is, preference minorities may be doubly disadvantaged, both as consumers and as citizens.

This chapter addresses this concern directly by asking whether the presence of Hispanic and black-targeted local media outlets affects whether targeted individuals turn out to vote. The recent history of Spanish-language television in Boston is telling. Between 1990 and 2000 the number of Hispanics in Massachusetts increased 50 percent, to 483,000. The Boston area is now 14 percent Hispanic and is the twenty-second-largest Hispanic market in the United States.[2] While Boston has had a local Spanish-language television station since 1993, the area had no Spanish-language local television news until 2003, when Univision affiliate WUNI launched Noticias Univision Nueva Inglaterra (Univision New England News).

Local Hispanics welcomed the station's launch of a daily local news show, feeling it long overdue. A local Puerto Rican radio host said, "It's about time . . . Because our presence now has changed in Massachusetts, there is a need for us . . . to get local news on a daily basis that addresses our concerns and issues."[3]

The arrival of local Spanish-language television news would improve the information flow to Boston-area Hispanics. As WUNI executive Meg Godin put it, "People whose native language is Spanish search for news in Spanish. They are finally able to tune into a news program that is geared directly to them. When we cover [the governor's] speech, we [will] find a Spanish-speaking spokesperson to speak for the administration and to our audience. We are going to make sure that our viewers will get the information they can appreciate."[4] Later Godin said, "We service an audience that doesn't go anywhere else for information . . . If we don't provide it, they won't get it. Now we are going to be able to give them their local news in Spanish." Indeed, the station promoted its local newscast with the slogan "News in your language."[5]

How might the availability of appealing media content affect whether people vote? It is not even clear why people vote in the first place.[6] In an electorate including millions of voters, the probability of affecting the outcome of an election is essentially nil. And voting has costs. Given the time it takes to become informed about the issues and candidates, as well as that needed to go to the polls and vote, a citizen placing value on both his time and the election outcome might well choose not to vote.

That said, many people do vote. Citizens obviously derive some benefit from the act of voting. It seems reasonable, if simplistic, to suppose that citizens choose whether to vote by comparing the benefit of participating (along with the infinitesimal benefit of raising their preferred candidate's win probability) against the cost of participation. In addition to the time spent actually voting, the main cost arises from the need to become informed. The availability of appealing media products with local information can play a role. To see this, imagine a blind and deaf citizen who has difficulty reading Braille. He would find it more difficult than his hearing and sighted counterparts to learn about issues and candidates, and he might therefore be less likely to vote.

Citizens who prefer Spanish to English-language media content provide a less remote example. A Spanish-language-preferring citizen living in a locale with few fellow Hispanics, and consequently facing no Spanish-language local media outlets, will find it harder to become informed. Compared with either his English-speaking local counterparts or Spanish-speaking persons in locales with larger Hispanic populations, he will face fewer, and less appealing, media options and might be less likely to vote. Likewise, a black citizen living in a metropolitan area with few blacks will face little local black-targeted media content and consequently may be less likely to vote.

It is important to note that media can affect citizens through either "content" or advertising. Even if the programming itself has no informational content, the availability of programming targeting a particular group allows advertisers to reach the group cost-effectively. Spending on political television advertising that targets Hispanics has become significant. In the 2004 presidential race, for example, John Kerry spent $1.3 million—and George W. Bush, $3.2 million—targeting Hispanic voters on Spanish-language television.[7]

How can I determine whether the availability of targeted media products, or lack thereof, affects voter turnout among blacks and Hispanics in local elections? First, I need data on the availability of targeted media outlets, by locale and over time. Second, I need information on whether people vote, by group (black, Hispanic, and so on), by locale, and over time.

With those pieces of information I could answer the question in a few different ways. First, do preference minorities turn out to vote more, relative to the rest of the population, in locales where the minority group in question has targeted local media products? Second, does the appearance of group-targeted local media outlets over time raise the tendency for group members to vote, relative to the time pattern for others? The investigation is shaped, as usual, by the availability of data and by institutional features, such as which media have outlets targeting which groups (for blacks, radio stations and weekly newspapers; for Hispanics, local television news), and which voting data are systematically available (turnout in general elections held in even-numbered years).[8]

Group-Targeted Media

Which media have group-targeted local outlets potentially relevant to voting? Until very recently there were very few metropolitan areas with group-targeted local daily newspapers. (Miami's Spanish-language *Nuevo Herald* is an exception.) And there is no specifically black-targeted local television news. But local Spanish-language news production and broadcast occurs in a substantial number of metropolitan areas. Indeed, in the past fifteen years there has been substantial growth in two major Spanish-language U.S. television networks, Univision and Telemundo. Both operate as national cable channels that are ubiquitously available in U.S. metropolitan areas. In addition, both networks have local affiliates that produce local news in a large and growing number of U.S. metropolitan areas.

Univision is the largest Spanish-language television network in the United States, operating "17 full-power and 7 low-power stations." National programming on the Univision Network "is also distributed through 56 broadcast television affiliates and 1,789 cable affiliates nationwide." Providing local as well as national (and international news) is a conscious company goal. According to the company, "Univision has the highest rated local news broadcasts among Hispanics in the U.S. Coverage has significantly increased over the years through investments in staff and facilities for reporting local news. Today, all of the Univision full-power stations broadcast local news twice every weeknight, and most also broadcast weekend local news." Because Univision dominates the Hispanic segment while affiliates of the English-language networks tend to split local audiences, Univision stations' local news is often dominant. "The Univision local news is the No. 1 rated overall newscast in many markets, including all audiences, both Hispanic and non-Hispanic."[9]

Univision reaches 98 percent of Hispanic television households, and it has more viewers than its largest competitor, "Telemundo, which reaches 91 percent of U.S. Hispanic viewers in 118 markets through its fifteen owned and operated stations, thirty-two broadcast affiliates, and nearly 450 cable affiliates. Telemundo is wholly owned by General Electric and is an operating subsidiary of NBC, the nation's leading broadcast network."[10] While the national programming of both Univision and Telemundo is widely available on cable systems, the two networks offer local news only in those metropolitan areas with the largest concentrations of Hispanics. By contacting all of the local affiliates currently operating, I obtained data on which metropolitan areas have local news broadcasts in Spanish, and when they began airing, 1994–2002. Both networks have grown substantially over the past fifteen years. In 1994, fourteen metropolitan areas among the 265 I studied had local Spanish-language television news. By 2002, the number had risen to twenty-five.

While there are very few black-targeted daily newspapers and no fully black-targeted local television broadcasts, there are dedicated black-targeted outlets in other media, in particular weekly newspapers and radio stations. As we saw in Chapter 3, black-targeted radio stations are present in some metropolitan areas and absent in others. The same is true for weekly newspapers. In addition to the data on Spanish-language local news, I also have data on black-targeted radio stations, by metropolitan area, in 1993 and 1997. In addition, I have data on black-targeted weekly newspapers at a single point in time, 1998.

Finally, I have information from the Current Population Survey (CPS) on general-election voter turnout for each of roughly 60,000 individuals who live in metro areas in each of the even-numbered years 1994–2002. These data allow me to ask how the availability of group-targeted media outlets affects the voter turnout of targeted preference minorities.

Spanish-Language Local Television News and Voting

How much does the availability of local television news in Spanish affect voter turnout? CPS data show that overall, voter turnout in even-numbered years varies between about two-thirds of eligible U.S. voters in presidential election years and half in other even-numbered years, when Congressional candidates and some state-wide (Senate and gubernatorial) races are the top of the ballot. Among Hispanics in the CPS, turnout varies between about half in presidential years and just over a third in other even-numbered years.[11]

The higher turnout in presidential election years stems from the heightened interest in the presidential contest, which in turn is supported by the uniformly high level of media coverage of the presidential contest in ubiquitous national media, particularly national television news.

What would we expect to find if local news in Spanish affects turnout? First, if Spanish-language local television news raises Hispanic turnout, then we should see higher turnout rates among Hispanics in metropolitan areas with Spanish-language local television news broadcasts than in areas without. Second, if the elevated Hispanic turnout is caused by Spanish-language local news, then the turnout of persons who do not watch Spanish-language news—non-Hispanics—should not be higher in places with local news in Spanish. Finally, this targeted local news should elevate Hispanic turnout, relative to non-Hispanic turnout, in elections that are not covered by national news media, which are available everywhere in English and Spanish. Thus, the increase in Hispanic voter turnout brought about by local Spanish television news should be larger in off-year (Congressional) elections and smaller in presidential elections.

The data in Table 4 confirm all three of these predictions. First, in the nonpresidential election years, Hispanic voter turnout is higher

TABLE 4 Hispanic and non-Hispanic voter turnout and the presence of Spanish-language local television news (percentages)

All Years Area has . . .	Hispanics	Non-Hispanics
No Spanish-language local news	36.8	58.2
Sample size	(5,441)	(173,328)
Spanish-language local news	45.2	59.8
Sample size	(11,732)	(79,330)

Nonpresidential election years (1994, 1998, 2002) Area has . . .	Hispanics	Non-Hispanics
No Spanish-language local news	30.8	52.9
Sample size	(3,265)	(107,837)
Spanish-language local news	40.0	54.5
Sample size	(7,235)	(49,565)

Presidential election years (1996, 2000) Area has . . .	Hispanics	Non-Hispanics
No Spanish-language local news	45.7	67.0
Sample size	(2,176)	(65,491)
Spanish-language local news	53.5	68.5
Sample size	(4,497)	(29,765)

Source: Calculations based on the Current Population Surveys, 1994–2002, described in more detail in Oberholzer-Gee and Waldfogel (2006).

Note: Panels show percentage of Hispanic and non-Hispanic population turning out to vote in places with and without Spanish-language local television news.

in the metropolitan areas with Spanish-language local news than in the locales without. Hispanic turnout averages 40 percent in locales with Hispanic local television news but only 31 percent in those without in nonpresidential years. In presidential years, Hispanic turnout in Spanish local news cities is 54 percent, compared with 46 percent in cities without.

Second, the turnout difference between metropolitan areas

with and without Hispanic Spanish-language local television news is negligible for non-Hispanic citizens. While the gap between Hispanic turnout in the locales with and without Spanish-language local television news was 8–11 percentage points, the gap for non-Hispanics was only 1–2 percentage points. Thus, the difference is not attributable to some determinant of voting common to both Hispanics and non-Hispanics. Finally, the effect is smaller, or nonexistent, in the presidential election years.

The data in Table 4—along with more sophisticated analyses—indicate that the presence of Spanish-language local television news raises turnout from an average of 31 percent to about 40 percent in nonpresidential election years, or by about a third. In presidential years, the presence of Spanish-language local television news raises Hispanic turnout about a sixth. These are large effects.

A second way to measure the effect of Spanish-language local news on Hispanic voter turnout is to ask how turnout changes over time in places that get a Spanish-language local newscast during the sample period. Of the metropolitan areas for which we have data on both Spanish news and voting over time, fourteen had Spanish-language local news in 1992 and twenty-five had it in 2002. Thus, Spanish news became available in eleven places over this period. What happened to the tendency for Hispanics to vote in these places? Studying this question is complicated by two factors. First, different places received Spanish-language local news at different times. Second, the elections of different years attracted different levels of interest. Analyzing these data requires a simple statistical model that explains the tendency for Hispanic individuals to vote as the sum of a metropolitan-area effect—an effect attributable to the election years, and a variable reflecting whether the metropolitan area has Spanish-language local news. We already know from the earlier analysis that Hispanics are more likely to vote in places with Spanish-language local news. The approach here asks a related but different question, whether the Hispanics in places that get a first Spanish-language local news station become more likely to vote.

Beyond the overall Hispanic time pattern of voter turnout, when a metro area gets Spanish-language local television news, Hispanic turnout increases five percentage points. As expected, in non-presidential years, the increase is an even-larger eight points, while the increase in presidential years is only two points (and not statistically discernible from zero). I can also examine effects on the non-Hispanic voting tendency, as a reality check. Given the ubiquity of English-language local television news, the presence or absence of Spanish-language local television news should have no effect on the non-Hispanic voting tendency. And indeed, there is no discernible change in non-Hispanic turnout with the local appearance of Spanish-language local television news.

The two approaches give very consistent estimates for the non-presidential years: an 8–11 percentage point boost in Hispanic voter turnout. The estimates reflect a large effect of Spanish-language local news on Hispanic voter turnout.

Effects of Black-Targeted Media on Voting

Do black-targeted radio stations and weekly newspapers affect black voter turnout? My data on these outlets are slightly less complete than the Spanish-language television data. I have the same voting data as before, but information on black-targeted radio stations in each locale is available at only two points in time, 1993 and 1997, and information on black weekly newspapers is known for only one year, 1998. Still, I can ask similar questions.[12]

Table 5 shows black and white voter turnout in 1998 in two groups of metropolitan areas, those with and those without black-targeted weekly newspapers, from the Current Population Survey. Turnout averages 41 percent among blacks in the metropolitan ar-

TABLE 5 Black and white voter turnout in locales with and without black-targeted weekly newspapers, 1998 (percentages)

	Black	White
Locales with black weeklies	52.8	53.2
Sample size	(4,532)	(25,014)
Locales without black weeklies	41.4	52.0
Sample size	(713)	(12,050)

Source: Calculated from Current Population Survey data combined with information on black-targeted newspapers, described in more detail in Oberholzer-Gee and Waldfogel (2005).

eas without a black weekly. By contrast, turnout averages 53 percent among blacks in metropolitan areas with at least one black-targeted weekly. Moreover, metropolitan areas with more than one or two black-targeted weekly newspapers have even higher rates of black voter turnout than those with fewer.

Does this difference reflect an effect of the presence of black-targeted media? It is always hard to be confident about attributing causality. For one thing, the relationship between elevated black turnout and black media outlets may reflect some other feature of the metropolitan areas related to both higher black turnout and the presence of black weeklies. A major factor supporting the causal interpretation, however, is the near absence of a white turnout differential between metropolitan areas with and without black-targeted weeklies (53 versus 52 percent).

How about black-targeted radio stations? We have data on the presence of black-targeted radio stations in each metropolitan area in both 1993 and 1997, two years that are nearly (but not exactly) aligned with the 1994 and 1998 election years. We can use these data, again in conjunction with the voter turnout data, to ask whether black turnout is higher in places with black radio. Indeed, it is. In both 1994 and 1998, blacks in metropolitan areas with black-targeted local radio stations have turnout rates of 49 and 53

TABLE 6 Black and white voter turnout in locales with and without black-targeted radio stations, 1994 and 1998 (percentages)

	1994		1998	
	Black	White	Black	White
locales with black radio stations	49.1	55.0	53.1	51.7
Sample size	(5,548)	(28,443)	(4,722)	(25,488)
locales without black radio stations	40.6	57.2	34.4	55.2
Sample size	(635)	(12,572)	(523)	(11,576)

Source: Described in more detail in Oberholzer-Gee and Waldfogel (2005).
Note: The voter turnout data refer to 1994 and 1998, while the radio station data cover 1993 and 1998.

percent, respectively, while blacks in metropolitan areas without black-targeted local radio turn out at rates of 40 and 34 percent, respectively (Table 6). White turnout rates are similar across places with and without black-targeted local radio. (In fact, white turnout is lower in the places with black-targeted local radio.)

Because I have data on the availability of black-targeted radio, by locale, at two points in time, we can ask whether the appearance of black-targeted radio, as happens in eleven of our sample metropolitan areas between 1994 and 1998, raises turnout among blacks, relative to whites. Estimates based on statistical models like those describing Hispanic voter turnout over time indicate that this is so. Black turnout increases by a large and significant sixteen percentage points in metropolitan areas that get a first black-targeted radio station, over and above the average growth in black turnout over this period of three percentage points. By contrast, white turnout changes only slightly in places that get a first black-targeted radio station. Hence, the growth in black turnout in locales that have launched a black-targeted radio station is not attributable to some more general phenomenon affecting both blacks and whites in those places.

In sum, the availability of group-targeted media outlets for local information, which markets deliver only to groups that are sufficiently large, increases those groups' turnout in local elections by large and statistically significant amounts.

Markets are inegalitarian both for traditional reasons—wealthier persons have more purchasing power and can afford more of the products that are available—and for the reason advanced in this book. When fixed costs are large and preferences differ across consumers, markets deliver products and satisfaction in rough proportion to disparate groups' sizes. Hence, we can add the numerous to the wealthy as those favored by the way that markets operate.

The political sphere is generally thought to be fundamentally different. The one-person, one-vote ideal is deeply ingrained. One of the "self-evident" Jeffersonian "truths" enshrined in the U.S. Declaration of Independence is "that all men are created equal." Regardless of a person's wealth, he or she could cast a ballot, at least by the mid-1960s. Of course, given the possible effects of other forms of political participation, such as campaign contributions, deviations from the one-person, one-vote ideal are already well understood.

The novel point in this chapter is that because of the way that media markets function, the same groups disadvantaged as consumers also find themselves disadvantaged as citizens. Market-provided media products influence individuals' decisions about whether to vote. Hence, those whom markets target with little or no information end up having less say as both consumers and citizens.

PART THREE

MARKET SOLUTIONS
AND THEIR LIMITS

CHAPTER 6

Market Enlargement
and Consumer Liberation

If the "who benefits whom" phenomenon is a problem, what are the solutions? My satisfaction depends on the mix of product preferences in the population when fixed costs are large relative to market size. The smaller are fixed costs in relation to market size, the greater the number of products that a market can accommodate. Hence the obvious solution, at least in theory, is to increase the size of the market relative to fixed costs.

Perhaps the simplest way to do so is through trade across geographic areas. Trade, the production in one locale for consumers there and elsewhere, expands markets. (By "trade" I do not necessarily mean international trade, just a geographical separation of production and consumption, including separations within a country.) Markets expanded by trade can support more products and greater product diversity for familiar reasons: Given the fixed costs required to make a product, a larger market can support more products. Indeed, unless fixed costs are very large—more on this in Chapters 7 and 8—then trade liberates consumers in both importing and exporting locales by promoting access to products at more points along the product spectrum introduced in Chapter 1.

The Liberating Effects of Trade

The liberating effects of trade on product variety are evident on any trip to the grocery store, mall, or discount store. To see the liberating effects of trade, imagine life on the U.S. frontier prior to the appearance of the Sears catalog in 1893.[1] With poor and infrequent shipping options, people had to make what they needed—food, clothing, building materials—locally, often within the family. Obviously, there were very few products available. Fast-forward to the present: consumers in any U.S. community large enough to support a Wal-Mart discount store have access to more than sixty thousand products shipped from around the globe.[2] The grocery nearest to most American consumers provides thousands of products that defy the place—and even the timing—of consumption. In the fall I can buy fresh apples from North American orchards, and in the spring I can buy them from South America. Almost regardless of where people choose to live, they have access to a wide range of products from around the world.[3]

The Chapter 1 framework can illustrate the liberating effects of trade. Consider a product whose characteristics vary along a single dimension, for example, inexpensive everyday white wines, which vary along a spectrum from dry to sweet. Prior to trade, each country has its domestic consumers and wine varieties. For concreteness, the places can be called Germany and France. For historical reasons, let's say that the majority of our "Germans" prefer wines near the sweet end of the spectrum, and German vintners accommodate local tastes by producing a wide variety of sweet wines but comparatively few dry whites. In the absence of trade, Germans favoring inexpensive sweet whites face many options—and derive great satisfaction—while German preference minorities favoring dry whites face few appealing options. The majority of our "French" consumers, by contrast, prefer white wines in the dry range. Most French consumers face options that they find appealing in the absence of trade, although French preference minorities preferring sweet wines do not.

Trade makes the products of each country available to the consumers of both countries. While trade might result in some shakeout—for example, French and German wines located exactly at the same point on the dry-sweet spectrum might not both survive—the basic effect of trade is to grant new product options to atypical French consumers wanting sweet wines and dry-loving Germans. As long as the number of product options available to consumers in each locale simply increases with trade, no one is worse off. Trade liberates the preference minorities who were previously isolated in places with few like-minded fellow consumers; they now have access to products closer to their ideal. The real-life experience of U.S. consumers in many industries confirms the liberating effects of trade.

Automobiles

In the 1960s, the Volkswagen Beetle reflected a preference of one group of U.S. consumers—the preference minority made up, in part, of hippies and intellectuals—for smaller vehicles before Detroit was making them. Consider American product offerings in the 1960s. A typical car weighed 3,500 pounds with a wheelbase of 119 inches. A VW Beetle, in contrast, weighed 1,786 pounds and had a wheelbase of only 95 inches.[4] One of the smallest cars made in Detroit was the Corvair at 2,450 pounds and with a 108-inch wheelbase. Pontiac's "senior compact car," the Tempest, was 2,970 pounds (and had a 116-inch wheelbase).[5] Presumably, Detroit was producing what most of America wanted. But not all of America. Many consumers were dissatisfied because the market brought forth few small car options that they found appealing.

In 1970, including imports (which accounted for one-sixth of U.S. auto sales), U.S. consumers could choose among 119 different car models. Although Japanese and European manufacturers produced many small-car options, the cars that were easily available to American consumers—from a dealer in town—were generally large. Consequently, a consumer interested in a small car had difficulty finding a car to suit his tastes. If the foreign small-car models had been available in the United States, they would have liberated the segment of U.S. consumers preferring small cars. By 2004, this access had been achieved: the import share had doubled to nearly a third, and U.S. consumers could choose from among over 275 different domestic and imported car models.[6] These cars ranged in size from very small European options such as the Smart or the Mini to the very large options such as the Humvee. Trade has thus increased the range of options available to U.S. consumers, liberating atypical American consumers from their fellow-citizens' tastes. Trade allows for the preference minority of U.S. consumers favoring small cars to benefit from the existence of European consumers favoring similar vehicles.

Television

During the 1964–1965 season, an American turning on the television on Thursday between 7:30 and 8:00 in the evening could choose among three programs: the *Flintstones* (a cartoon about a "modern stone-aged family") the *Munsters* (about "a loving family of misfits who reside in a spooky cobweb-filled house at 1313 Mockingbird Lane") and the first half of *Daniel Boone* (featuring the adventures of the legendary Kentucky frontiersman).[7] While these programs appealed to many—the *Flintstones* and the *Munsters* were among the top twenty shows in the Nielsen ratings during the 1960–1961 and 1964–1965 seasons, respectively—these shows and others on the air were quite unappealing to many others, perhaps first and foremost because there was very little ethnic or racial diversity on the air during the 1960s.[8] But racial minorities were not the only audiences underserved by the three networks. A quick review of the top twenty network offerings for any season during the 1960s indicates that the vast majority of shows aimed for the "middle of the market." Consequently, sophisticated consumers were a preference minority particularly disenchanted with television. President John F. Kennedy's appointee as FCC Chairman, Newton Minow, declared television in 1961 to be "a vast wasteland."[9] From the perspective of many consumers, television's offerings were a three-choice tyranny of the majority.

Forty years later, the landscape has changed substantially. Rather than three options, most consumers have access to at least fifty stations on their local cable systems.[10] Satellite systems offer more. Dish Network's Everything Pak includes "over 230 channels of great television."[11] The vast majority of cable channels do not carry local content. Rather, they carry specialized content of interest to particular groups of people.

Does the wide variety of national programming on cable and satellite liberate consumers with diverse tastes? I get some clues on my daily commute to work, which takes me through a low-income and heavily black Philadelphia neighborhood of rowhouses called Mantua. According to the 2000 Census, this neighborhood (Census tract 109) is over 90 percent black, and the median family income is $15,543 per year. Only 14 percent of the adults have more than a high-school education, and nearly half of families (44 percent) live below the poverty line.[12] Virtually every outward sign of wealth and success is less prevalent in Mantua than in the more affluent suburb where I live. Except one. There is, to my eye, a surprisingly large number of satellite television dishes perched outside the Mantua rowhouses, far more per household than I see in my high-income, predominantly white suburb.

The Mantua neighborhood of Philadelphia is not alone in its flowering of satellite dishes. Ian Buruma writes that neighborhoods like Overtoomse Veld in Amsterdam, "inhabited almost entirely by immigrants, mainly people of Moroccan or Turkish origin, . . . are often called 'dish cities,' because of the many satellite dishes picking up TV stations in North Africa and the Middle East."[13]

To what do Mantua and Overtoomse Veld owe the "dish city" distinction? Satellite TV services carry a large variety of programming, including some channels not otherwise available locally. For example, in addition to Black Entertainment Television (BET), which is also available on many cable systems, DirecTV carries a number of channels not available on local cable that might appeal to black viewers: Black Starz (a premium channel that is "the first and only movie channel dedicated to showcasing black artists 24 hours a day, seven days a week"), The Word ("Free to all customers. Multi-denominational urban religious programming with both spiritual and educational content"), and Daystar ("Free to all customers. The fastest growing Christian network in America. Interdenominational and multicultural, Daystar features the nation's leading ministries. More live remote broadcasts of major Christian events than any other network.")[14]

DirecTV also carries specialized channels appealing to other individuals who are sometimes without local compatriots. For example, it offers BYU-TV ("Non-commercial educational material from Brigham Young University's 3 campuses. Programming also includes BYU sports, devotionals, concerts and education week broadcasts from BYU and LDS General Conference"), which appeals to Mormon viewers, and Galavision's Spanish-language entertainment programming.

Of course, satellite television subscription is just a more visible, and slightly more extreme, version of cable television, which also allows access to a variety of programming—including programming targeted at some specific groups—that is not available locally over the air. While analog cable typically provides access to at least fifty channels, satellite and digital cable offer access to hundreds. Satellite dishes evoke a mental image of individuals surrounded by inhospitable local information options and seeking liberation from the local paucity via content provided for national, or international, audiences.

More systematic evidence is available that consumers turn to national television offerings for liberation. For example, in Chapter 3 we saw that black and Hispanic consumers face less appealing local television programming as they, respectively, make up smaller shares of the local metropolitan area population. In such circumstances, do they instead turn to national programming? A study I conducted for the Federal Communications Commission in 2002 asked whether minorities use cable and satellite television more if they live in metropolitan areas with smaller black population shares. I found that the lower the share of local population that is black, the more cable television channels that blacks use. For example, in a metropolitan area that is 50 percent black, blacks regularly use roughly seven cable channels, while in an area that is only 5 percent black, blacks use more than eight, on average. The numbers for Hispanics are similar. Hispanics in an area that is half Hispanic use an average of about five cable channels, while Hispanics isolated in areas that are only 5 percent Hispanic regularly watch an average of seven.[15] By contrast, in places with heavily black (or Hispanic) local populations, blacks and Hispanics spend more time watching the programming offered on local television. We can say, based on this evidence, that as persons are surrounded by fewer persons sharing their preferences, they are more likely to find national programming a solution to their isolation. As the satellite dishes in Mantua and Overtoomse Veld suggest, the market enlargement brought about by cable and satellite television liberates consumers from their neighbors' tastes.

While isolated minorities use cable and satellite more when they have less appealing local television options, it is impossible to say whether their greater use of national information fully offsets the lower satisfaction that their local options provide. What's more, the substitution of national for local media products may leave them less engaged in local communities (just as the absence of local group-targeted programming reduces political participation). So the liberation that national television offers preference minorities, while real, may not be complete; that is, it may not fully overcome the dissatisfaction with local programming.

Internet

Like cable and satellite television, the Internet enlarges markets by making information, as well as retail goods, available to consumers around the country (and world). Do preference minorities turn to the Internet for liberation from unappealing product options available locally? What sorts of sites might liberate preference minorities? Retail Internet sites, like mail-order catalogues before them, provide one clear possibility: a person who has no store nearby can instead buy online or from a catalog. Even when there's a store nearby, the online store generally offers more variety. The Sears store nearest to my house, at one of the largest shopping malls in the United States (the King of Prussia Mall), sells Lands' End pants, which are sized by their waistlines and lengths. Online, I can order pants with waistlines in even or odd numbers of inches, and the inseams are adjustable to quarter-inch increments, giving me countless combinations of waistlines and inseams. Sears at King of Prussia stocks only even-numbered waistlines, and inseams of one-inch increments, giving me a choice among a tenth as many sizes in each color. And few of the conceivable combinations are actually in stock.[16] Even for a shopper in an affluent suburb of Philadelphia, the range of choice online is large and liberating compared with what is available nearby.

These liberating effects are not limited to retail but extend to information and entertainment as well. For example, some streaming music sites offer over one hundred channels of music programming, over twice the number provided by radio stations in even the largest U.S. markets. Internet radio—and for that matter satellite radio—may appeal to listeners in both large and small markets, but presumably provides more of a benefit to listeners whose tastes make them preference minorities locally, and who therefore face few suitable local radio stations. News sites such as CNN.com or MSNBC.com present domestic and international news of interest to individuals in cities of all sizes. But because small markets tend to have slender local newspapers with few local or national stories, people who live in them may place a higher value on the availability of news on the Internet.

How acutely a consumer craves liberation will depend not only on the total number of persons in her local market, but also on the number of like-minded persons in her local market. We have seen extensive evidence that blacks and whites tend to have different preferences in media products. We can determine whether the Internet liberates preference minorities using evidence on whether blacks are more likely to connect to the Internet when they comprise a smaller fraction of the local market. That is, is there systematic evidence for the "dish city" effect in Internet use?

This test is complicated somewhat by what has come to be known as the "digital divide." As of 2000, black households connected to the Internet at 46 percent of the white rate. Because connection requires computer ownership and the shouldering of access charges—and because blacks have lower incomes than whites—some of this gap is to be expected. But even after statistically adjusting for income and education, at least two-thirds of the raw racial gap remains.[17]

Of course, even if equal shares of white and black populations were online, the white online audience would be nearly ten times larger. We would therefore expect a lot more and perhaps better content targeting whites than blacks, much in the manner that larger metropolitan areas have more or better media products appealing to the dominant group. If content helps to attract people online, then blacks would find less appealing content and might therefore be less likely to connect. Still, relative to this gap, we can ask whether isolated blacks have a higher tendency to connect compared with blacks in areas with large local black populations.

To explore this question I use data from the U.S. government's 2000 Current Population Survey to ask how the black and white tendencies to connect to the Internet vary among individuals in different metropolitan areas with different proportions of black and white residents.[18] After accounting for individual determinants of the tendency to connect such as income and education, black people are less likely to connect as their markets have more blacks and are more likely to connect as their markets have more whites. The white connection tendency does not vary across metropolitan areas with the mix of blacks and whites. How large are the estimated relationships? In a market with the ninetieth percentile black share (over a quarter black, or 0.273), blacks would be 20.2 percentage points less likely than whites to be connected (0.1649 + 0.2733 * 0.1363), while in a market with the tenth percentile black share (less than 2 percent, or 0.0195), blacks would be 16.8 percentage points less likely to be connected. While there is a digital divide, the divide shrinks in markets where blacks are isolated.

In sum, the trade in information brought about by the Internet and national television, like international trade in automobiles, provides liberation to those preference minorities who have few domestic products nearby to their liking. As with cable and satellite, the liberation enabled by the Internet entails the substitution of nonlocal for local information sources. Still, as the examples of automobiles, television, and the Internet show, market enlargement can give isolated consumers access to a wider range of products. Market enlargement is thus a force providing product market liberation to preference minorities.

Before celebrating the liberation that trade information enables—over cable, satellite, and the Internet—we should keep two things in mind. First, the effects are small. That is, the extent to which consumers use national sources of information when local ones are absent is modest. Second, consumers reap different benefits from nonlocal and local sources. For example, in Chapter 5 we saw that local news affects voting in local elections. Consumers turning to nonlocal sources when local sources are unappealing will be less engaged in local affairs.

CHAPTER 7

Fixed Costs, Product Quality, and Market Size

Residents of Fergus Falls, Minnesota (population 13,000), and the Minneapolis–St. Paul metropolitan area (population roughly three million) face very different product options. For some products, such as restaurants, bigger places like Minneapolis have more (and more varied) options, including a wider range of qualities.

Fergus Falls has thirty-six restaurants, including two Burger Kings, one McDonald's, a Pizza Hut, a Domino's, a Subway, and an Applebee's. But if you want to eat at TGI Friday's, or California Pizza Kitchen, or Romano's Macaroni Grill, or Chili's, not to mention Morton's Steakhouse, you will not find them in Fergus Falls. Nor will you find there a kosher deli, an Afghan or vegetarian restaurant, or a locally produced bagel. Some of these products—Chili's and TGI Friday's—are available fifty miles away in the 172,000-person metro area of Fargo, North Dakota. But most are beyond the distance a person would normally drive for a meal.

Some 180 miles from Fergus Falls, Minneapolis has more than four thousand restaurants, including scores of chain restaurants like McDonald's, Applebee's, and Chili's. Minneapolis also has Zagat-rated restaurants in thirty-two different cuisines, including both vegetarian and vegan, as well as "restaurants from every corner of the globe, from Tibet to Nigeria, and Ecuador to Russia."[1] Larger markets liberate restaurant patrons; more demand renders consumers "free to choose" among more alternatives, including those closer to their favorites, particularly—as we saw in Chapter 4—if they are willing to travel a few miles.

In other product categories, the larger Minneapolis does not have many more products; rather, it has different—and in some sense better—products. Daily newspapers provide a prime example. The Minneapolis–St. Paul area has two major daily newspapers, the Minneapolis *Star Tribune* and the St. Paul *Pioneer Press*. The *Star Tribune* is by far the dominant paper, particularly in Minneapolis, and has a paid circulation of 380,000 (compared with 190,000 for the *Pioneer Press*). The *Star Tribune* employs 189 writers and editors to produce a paper that averages seventy-seven pages in length each day (excluding Sunday). Fergus Falls has a single daily paper, the Fergus Falls *Daily Journal,* a roughly ten-page paper produced by five reporters, one photographer, and an editor.

The Minneapolis–St. Paul metropolitan area has 220 times the population of Fergus Falls. Yet although Minneapolis has more than one hundred times as many restaurants as Fergus Falls, it does not have many more newspapers. Rather, Minneapolis has a newspaper with more content that is more costly to produce. Greater market size provides consumers more freedom of choice among restaurants. Having more people in my metropolitan area (and especially in my neighborhood, as Chapter 4 shows) benefits consumers by raising the number—and variety—of restaurants nearby. More people nearby benefits consumers in the newspaper market as well, but in a different way. It makes the metropolitan area's paper bigger and perhaps better, but additional demand does not provide consumers with more choices. If the way the paper is targeted—by, say, writing style, or topical coverage—appeals to me, then a lengthier paper makes me better off. If I don't care for the targeting—if, for example, I prefer hard or soft news, or Spanish to English language text—then the product improvements brought about by more demand do not help me.

That trade and market expansion tend to liberate consumers is immediately evident during any trip to the mall or grocery store. Even in small, geographically isolated areas, at least in small metropolitan areas, consumers can choose among thousands of products that are created with large, possibly global, markets and are transported to local stores everywhere. But the corrective powers of market expansion and trade are not unlimited. While larger markets liberate consumers in some product categories—the basic who-benefits-whom mechanism at work—this liberation is incomplete in other categories. When do larger markets bring about more freedom of choice, and when do they not?

The Benefit of Increased Market Size

Larger markets tend to have more product variety. With the same setup costs as the smaller market, they can support more varieties, packed closer together. In this way—through product proliferation—larger markets promote consumer satisfaction. This was the mechanism by which larger metropolitan areas produced greater satisfaction though radio markets. Minneapolis has enough jazz fans to support a commercial jazz station; Fargo, North Dakota, does not.

So, what's the hitch? When do larger markets fail to experience product proliferation? Crucial to this mechanism is the assumption that fixed costs do not increase—or at least not much—as market size increases. If fixed costs rise with market size, then the number of products—and the distance (along the color line) to the nearest product—need not decline as market size rises.

Why would fixed costs rise with market size in differentiated product markets? The major reason is that expenditures on fixed costs can improve quality. And when consumers largely agree on what constitutes quality, then firms can find it in their interest to invest more in quality in larger markets.[2] A newspaper sold to a population of one million can "afford" more writers than one selling to only ten thousand. Similarly, producers of a movie made for a world audience of perhaps a billion persons in the United States, Europe, and Japan can "afford" to spend more on actors and special effects. Producers can improve the quality of different products in different ways, and some examples best illustrate the point.

Fixed costs, as we've seen, are those that are not directly affected by the number of units produced or sold. Research and development (R&D) and advertising are two basic ways of improving quality through fixed costs. R&D and advertising might seem an odd pair since R&D generates tangible product improvements while advertising operates by shaping consumers' perceptions. From a market standpoint, however, they serve the same function: they increase consumers' willingness to buy a product through expenditures on fixed costs that, once the product is made, do not raise the cost of serving an additional consumer.

The particular industries I have discussed in this book differ in the processes that produce quality. The quality of local media products is based exclusively on fixed costs. The cost of media-content producers (reporters, editors, on-air talent, and so on), who collectively determine the quality of these products, does not vary with the number of readers, listeners, or viewers.[3]

Daily newspapers provide one vivid example. The nature of daily newspapers varies substantially across metropolitan areas. Larger metropolitan areas have systematically larger—and in many ways, better—products. The single paper in Fergus Falls, the ten-page or so *Daily Journal*, has never won a Pulitzer Prize. The Philadelphia *Inquirer*, by contrast, which serves a metropolitan area of nearly five million persons and has an average daily paid circulation of 357,000, averages seventy pages in length and has won eighteen Pulitzer Prizes in its history. The *Inquirer* is, by many measures, a better product than the *Daily Journal*.

These two examples illustrate a more general relationship. In this industry, larger metropolitan areas do not mainly have more products. Rather, larger metropolitan areas mainly have higher-quality products, which are more costly to produce. How does a larger market support a single—or just a few—major product(s) rather than a host of smaller varieties? After all, if Fergus Falls can support a daily newspaper with a population of around thirteen thousand, then the Minneapolis area, with a population of almost three million, could in principle support over two hundred daily newspapers. Yet it has essentially two. This stunning failure of product proliferation with increased market size is repeated in every large U.S. metro area. Even the largest U.S. metropolitan area, New York City, has only three or four dailies that target the entire metro area (the *Times,* the *Post,* the *Daily News,* and perhaps Long Island's *Newsday*). Counting all suburban dailies published in the consolidated metropolitan area that includes suburbs in Connecticut and New Jersey, as well as New York, the area has eleven daily newspapers, although the top three account for 54 percent of the total metro-area newspaper circulation.[4] That larger markets have larger and more costly newspapers, rather than many more newspapers, is borne out by systematic analysis. Both newspaper length (in pages) and newspaper staffs increase steadily with growth in market size.

Because additional quality in newspapers is achieved through expenditures on fixed costs rather than additional per-copy, or "variable," costs, a firm making a better product need not charge a higher price than its lower-quality competitor. If consumers, or most consumers, agree on what constitutes quality, then they will prefer the better paper essentially en masse. In this way, the process of quality competition can cause a market to have few products, even though the market is very large.

Of course, this situation only arises if sufficient numbers of consumers agree on what constitutes quality. If consumers have sharply different preferences, for example over language (English versus Spanish), they would not agree on what constitutes quality. A well-written and universally fascinating article in English is of no value to a person who reads only Spanish. Indeed, this is why in the 1990s the *Miami Herald* split into two distinct products, the *Miami Herald* and *el Nuevo Herald*.

What other markets share this feature of daily newspaper markets, in which quality is produced with fixed rather than variable costs? Movies are a clear example. The quality of a film is in its writing, acting, and directing, rather than its physical copies. Once a film is made and marketed, the studio incurs no additional cost when an additional person views the movie. True, the studio must make more prints to allow the movie to be shown on more screens. And the studio must burn more DVDs if more individuals are to see it by buying or renting a personal copy. But these costs are small compared with the costs of producing and advertising the movie. Other examples include pharmaceutical products, software, and magazines. In all of these industries, the number of products available is not proportional to the revenue available.

Restaurants produce quality in a very different way than newspapers. Of course, restaurants also differ from newspapers in that they are differentiated by cuisine and geography, not simply by quality. But even within cuisine and geography, much of the quality difference across restaurants is due to differences in the quality of ingredients and labor, both of which are variable costs. Preparing an additional dish requires additional food and additional chef labor in a way that delivering another copy of the newspaper or sending a radio signal to an additional receiver does not.

Because higher-quality restaurants have per-meal higher costs of labor and ingredients, high- and low-quality restaurants can coexist in the market in a way that varied daily newspapers cannot. For example, veal costs more than ground beef; and higher-quality restaurants attract a clientele willing to pay high prices for veal dishes, while lower-quality restaurants attract those willing to pay less for hamburger. In strong contrast to the newspaper example, because of their more costly inputs, the higher-quality restaurants cannot undercut the prices of their lower-quality rivals. As a result, the market supports a range of options. And a larger market supports a larger range of choices for consumers, including more restaurants of varying prices and qualities. As we have seen earlier, larger markets—at all levels of geography—have proportionately more restaurants. That is, a market twice as large has twice as many restaurants.

For products where larger markets do not have more products than smaller markets, are consumers no better off? Not at all. The setup we are discussing has two forms of differentiation. The first is the position along the line representing, for example, shirt color or language (English versus Spanish). The second is quality, say number of articles or page length. Suppose there are two types of readers who differ by whether they prefer a paper in English or Spanish. Newspapers can be in English or Spanish, and everyone prefers a paper with more articles, provided it's in his preferred language. Then even though a larger market does not have more dailies in English, it has longer English dailies. So most people—English-speakers—in larger markets get a product they prefer to the product they would face in a smaller market.

While market expansion helps to promote the provision of additional products catering to the a diversity of tastes, there is a limit to how much it solves the problem of consumers with unusual tastes when quality is produced with fixed costs.

This is really just a variant of the "who benefits whom" theme. When fixed costs are small, more people benefit me by helping to bring forth a greater proliferation of products. When additional people share my preferences more closely, they help to bring forth varieties that I particularly like.

For products like newspapers, where larger markets do not bring about a proliferation of products but rather bigger products, additional people still can benefit me, but the mechanism is different.

They help to make the product bigger. If I like its targeting, then their presence benefits me more. The further my tastes lie from the norm—for example, if I speak only Spanish and the paper is in English—the less I benefit from the presence of additional potential or actual consumers.

CHAPTER 8

Trade and the Tyranny
of Alien Majorities

In a memorable gesture during the 1999 World Trade Organization meetings in Seattle, antiglobalization demonstrators vandal-
ized McDonald's outlets and broke windows at Starbucks.[1] Among
the many complaints of opponents of globalization is distress over
global exporting of branded U.S. products such as Coke, McDonald's, and Nike.[2]

But what, exactly, do the opponents of globalization oppose about
the availability of U.S. products abroad? After all, as I argued earlier, the availability of additional products could simply provide
foreign consumers with more options, thereby offering preference
minorities liberation through trade. But is it that simple? Does trade
simply increase the number of options available to foreign consumers? Or does trade crowd out local culture and ways of life as
well? In a world without fixed costs, where a product is viable regardless of how few people want it, the introduction of trade simply
increases the number of product options available to consumers.
But in industries where fixed costs are substantial, domestic products each require threshold levels of demand for viability. As a
result, importing products suited to "alien majorities"—the consumers determining product targeting in some distant place—can
alter a country's domestic products. Domestic products might shift
their positioning or be withdrawn. Exporting, too, can alter the ex-

porter's products if the few available products shift toward the tastes of foreign, or alien, majorities. A few vignettes help to illustrate these concerns.

France versus Hollywood

During a protracted trade negotiation, France and the rest of Europe held firm on their right to protect domestic artistic industries against the threat of U.S. domination. Under the "cultural exception," as it is known, France taxes all film box-office receipts (foreign and domestic) at 11 percent to provide subsidies to French film production. These subsidies, along with other government support, provide a substantial share of the revenue of the French domestic film industry.

Economists are generally critical of trade barriers, seeing behind them a domestic industry that has figured out how to earn higher profits by forestalling foreign competition.[3] In the United States we are no strangers to this phenomenon. The United States limits imports of low-cost cane sugar, which largely come from poor equatorial countries, which in effect raises the profits of domestic beet and cane sugar producers. By some estimates these restrictions cost U.S. consumers $2.4 billion per year and benefit U.S. producers by $1.0 billion per year.[4]

But in the story about French film, the ostensible purpose of the French film subsidies is not chiefly to protect French producers but rather to protect French consumers' culture. According to a French member of the European parliament, "France, supported by other countries such as Canada, was worried about the risk of invasion of its territory by these American 'products,' not only for economic reasons (our balance of trade was already showing a large deficit), but for cultural reasons and reasons to do with national identity, the danger being that we would see the inhabitants of our country progressively adopting American ways of thinking and their approach to life."[5] No comparable argument can be made for U.S. protection of the domestic sugar industry. Equatorial cane and domestic sugars have an identical taste, so there is no sense in which, say, domestic confectionary or soft drink culture is preserved by this policy.

What are the French worried about? Presumably that Hollywood movies would divert demand from French cinema. And why would this be a problem? Well, films are a prime example of a high fixed cost product. If Hollywood films divert enough demand from French fare, then much of the French fare will not be viable. Some of the products available prior to trade would be unavailable once trade occurs and once many French consumers forsake work by their native directors for Hollywood films. Is there any merit to this argument?

Hollywood versus the Rest of the World

At least since World War II, the United States has been the bogeyman of world culture, exporting cultural products that many around the world find vulgar. As we have seen in previous chapters, the larger the market that, say, a film, targets, the greater the investment that the film warrants. The United States has a large home market and as a result, Hollywood movies involve larger budgets (bigger stars, more explosions) than do films of other countries. Other countries, whose movies target small domestic audiences, cannot compete in terms of sheer spectacle with Hollywood productions.[6] From the European perspective, the arrival of U.S. films constitutes a particular kind of tyranny of the majority; it is the tyranny of an alien majority, one composed of U.S. consumers and their vulgar tastes.

As recently as the 1980s, U.S. films were tailored to American tastes and then, as an afterthought, distributed to (that is, dumped on) foreign markets. Until recently the United States has been the perpetrator—while Asia and particularly Europe perceive themselves as "victims"—in the globalization of the film industry. Recently, however, the tables have turned. U.S. film producers are now fully cognizant of the international market, which for many U.S. movies generates the majority of revenue. Hollywood has recently begun to take international audiences into account when deciding which movies to make in the first place. Action movies export particularly well, especially to Japan. So American audiences are finding that Hollywood's film mix has shifted away from domestic preferences and toward the tastes of foreign audiences. For the first time, U.S. consumers are the victims of product market globalization, as our own domestic products are changing to suit the needs of foreigners. It is an unfamiliar and unwelcome change for U.S. audiences.

Significantly, these phenomena are all linked by a simple common cause—fixed costs that remain high relative to even world markets.

Trade and the Tyranny of Alien Majorities

In Chapter 6 we saw, in our simple framework, how trade can liberate consumers as the fixed costs of products shrink relative to the enlarged world market. When fixed costs are substantially higher—and potentially higher still when trade is allowed—the effects of trade can be more complicated. To illustrate the possible effects, consider an industry with high fixed costs such as big-budget, would-be-blockbuster movies. To make things simple, suppose that fixed costs are high enough so that there is only one product (one such movie released, say, per month). Suppose too that movies can only be made in a range that spans drama to action. In the absence of trade, the firm producing domestically targets a typical domestic consumer, whose ideal movie is, say, nearer to drama than action.

In this scenario, one of two things can happen. First, the studio making the product can begin exporting the product to foreign audiences, as when Hollywood targets a global, rather than simply an American, audience. Second, the products from elsewhere can become available in the domestic market, as when Hollywood movies become available in France, or the *New York Times* becomes available in local U.S. markets.

Let's first discuss these two possibilities in theory. First, suppose that Hollywood discovers a potential global audience with preferences that are not identical to American preferences. To be precise, the international viewers whose preferences matter to Hollywood's targeting decisions are the persons who would be willing to watch a "big American movie," and they dislike dialogue and favor action. A producer seeking the largest global audience (including Americans) will target his movie more toward action than a typical domestic consumer's ideal. This new movie delivers more satisfaction to those among the Americans who are action-hungry, but it delivers less satisfaction to drama-oriented Americans, who become less likely to patronize the offered fare. The action-oriented elements of international audiences are of course happier with the new American movie. The result is that becoming an exporter can change the positioning of some domestic products, to the benefit of some domestic consumers and the detriment of others.

The recent history of Hollywood is consistent with this characterization. As recently as twenty years ago, when U.S. film producers made movies, their intended audience was domestic. While they garnered some revenue from foreign countries, they did not target their films to the preferences of international viewers. Those viewers were, instead, simply expected to appreciate U.S. fare. As Sherry Lansing, Paramount's chairwoman, put it: "When I worked as a producer and we made 'Fatal Attraction' in the mid-80s, we never even thought of the global audience. Back then we thought, 'If it does well in America, it will do well overseas.'"[7]

The more recent availability of an international audience, in addition to the U.S. domestic market, provides an example of market expansion through trade. Whatever number of films the potential audience in the United States can support per year, the United States with Europe and Japan can collectively support even more. According to Lynn Hirschberg, writing in the *New York Times Magazine,* "The expected audience for nearly all American-made studio movies, the audience they are designed and created for, has shifted from the 50 states to the global marketplace."[8] On its face, this trend simply adds to the demand, and therefore the supply of available films, which would seem to make everyone better off.

But the situation is not that simple. U.S. and international film preferences are different, and film is an industry in which the size of the investment that a project warrants depends on the size of the audience a studio can hope to capture. With the expectation of a global audience, a producer can profitably invest a great deal more. But in order to effectively target an international audience, Hollywood must position its products differently than it would if domestic producers were seeking only an American audience. According to Hirschberg, "nuances of language or the subtleties of comedy do not translate easily between cultures, but action or fantasy or animation is immediately comprehensible, even if you live in, say, Japan, which is the country that most big studios long to reach. Films like this year's "Troy" (which was shown at Cannes), "The Day After Tomorrow" and "Van Helsing," which are not dependent on dialogue, did not play as well as expected in America but became huge hits in many other countries, making several times what they made in the U.S. box office."[9]

Dialogue is not the only casualty of Hollywood's global aspirations. For example, films based on U.S. sports, films expressing pro-American sentiments, and even films with American stars may face resistance in the international box office. According to Nina Jacobsen, president of Buena Vista at Disney, "You have to realize that if you put a sports movie into production, it will do disastrously internationally. It won't travel no matter how good it is, so you adjust the budget accordingly. The world just doesn't care about other people's sports."[10]

Or Lansing again: "It's hard, for instance, to pick a villain with a global audience in mind." As Hirschberg put it, "Strangely, politics, especially anti-American politics, just might have global appeal." Finally, "Today's global audience, it seems, has little interest in the next generation of American leading men . . . Tom Cruise or Brad Pitt may still draw crowds, but the world's newest stars come from other English-language-speaking countries, like Ireland (Colin Farrell), England (Jude Law, Clive Owen), Scotland (Ewan McGregor), or Australia (Russell Crowe)."[11]

While some U.S. film consumers—perhaps those favoring action over dialogue and those favoring sinister American characters—are made better off by Hollywood's attempts to target world preferences, others are made worse off. In this context, as in others, trade creates winners and losers, even among consumers.

If fixed costs were low, then the availability of a new audience would increase the range of products offered, leaving the existing (domestic-targeted) options in place. But because fixed costs are high, the new audience actually shifts the targeting of the big-budget movies that get made. It is true that Hollywood produces many films per year. A wide range of small-scale films, in addition to the big-budget spectacles, are offered, so many niche audiences continue to find some products. But the targeting of costly movies has changed.

Importing and the Tyranny of Alien Majorities

What does importing do? For example, how does the availability of Hollywood fare affect the film industries of importing countries? Or, to take a domestic U.S. example of intercity trade, how does national distribution of the *New York Times* affect local newspaper markets? Before analyzing this case systematically, a story about New Haven, Connecticut, may be instructive.

New Haven is the heart of a larger metropolitan area stretching from Orange to Meriden, with a total population of half a million.[12] As the last stop on the Metro North commuter train from New York City, the city is the boundary between New York and New England. New Haven is also the home of Yale University, and the area is quite well educated. Nearly a third of the residents of the New Haven–Meriden area have a bachelor's degree or more education, compared with only a quarter for the country as a whole.[13] The area is served by the *New Haven Register,* a daily newspaper with a circulation of nearly 100,000 and a readership of over 200,000.[14]

I lived in New Haven in the early 1990s, and I was puzzled by what struck me as an inane focus of the newspaper. I distinctly remember a banner headline declaring about the weather, "It's Hot!" Why would the newspaper for a sizable metropolitan area that is home to one of the world's major research institutions and a large college-educated population give such prominent place—a banner headline, above the fold—to information that is news to no one?

After living in New Haven for a while, I realized that most of my Yale colleagues did not read the *Register.* Instead—since, like me, they were not natives of Southern Connecticut and had no special interest in local affairs—they read the *New York Times.* I wondered: if the *Register* ceded the elite market to the *Times,* would that cause them to focus on content appealing to the people not inclined to purchase the *Times?* In short, did the *New York Times* make the *New Haven Register* a paper that focused more on lightweight topics like the weather?

Our framework is well suited to analyzing this example. Imagine a product spectrum describing the amount of local news coverage. A national product, such as the *New York Times,* has two features relevant to this discussion. First, it is less local than the local product. Second, it is of higher quality than the local product. In our framework, this means that people don't necessarily patronize the nearest local product; the higher quality of the national product will incline a person whose ideal degree of local content is equidistant between the imported and the local product to purchase the national product.

Local firms in any market target typical local consumers. When the *New York Times* becomes available, local consumers who either care less about local coverage, or particularly value high-quality national reporting, switch to the *Times*. In response to having lost its most nationally oriented consumers, the local paper repositions itself to attract some very locally oriented consumers, including some who previously did not read a paper. While most consumers are made better off by the availability of the imported product, some consumers—those who preferred the old local paper to either the *Times* or the local paper as it was retargeted—are made worse off by its arrival and by the associated local product's shift to more local coverage. In short, the availability of an imported product benefits many of the consumers who choose it. But it also changes the targeting of the domestic product, making some consumers better off and others worse off.

There is systematic evidence about the effect on local papers and their readers of the availability of the *New York Times*. The *Times* has pursued national distribution for the past twenty, and especially the past ten, years. National circulation now accounts for over half of the *Times*'s circulation. The *Times* is now available for home delivery ("by 7 AM") in over two hundred metropolitan areas around the United States. Its effects on local consumers and on the targeting of local newspapers corroborate the predictions from this framework.

How does the availability of the *Times* affect local markets? The *Times* targets college-educated consumers, and when it is available, many college-educated consumers subscribe to the *Times* rather than the local paper. Zip-code-level data on local newspaper circulation and population characteristics, along with metropolitan area data on *Times* circulation for 1996–2000, show that metropolitan areas with higher *Times* circulation growth during the mid-1990s experienced reductions in local paper use among educated consumers, relative to their less-educated counterparts.[15] Presumably, the more educated consumers find the appeal of high-quality national and international coverage stronger than the pull of more local coverage.

Given the loss of these consumers, the local paper repositions itself toward more local coverage. Data on the topical assignment of reporters at newspapers in each metropolitan area show that during the mid-1990s, local papers in metropolitan areas where the *Times* made larger inroads repositioned their coverage toward more local content. More than in metro areas with little growth in *Times* penetration, they increased the fraction of reporting devoted to local issues and reduced the fraction covering national and international topics. As a result of their repositioning, local papers in markets with more *Times* growth actually added circulation among less-educated persons.

Again, trade benefited many consumers. Former nonreaders who take up either the repositioned local paper or the *Times* are clearly better off (with something rather than nothing). But there are both winners and losers among both products' patrons (the *Times* consumers and consumers of the repositioned local paper). All readers of the repositioned local papers prefer it to the *Times*—that's why they chose as they did—but some of them would have been even more satisfied if that local paper had not changed direction. Similarly, all *Times* readers are more satisfied with the *Times* than the repositioned local paper, but some of those readers would have preferred the old local paper over the *Times*. The point, again, is that with large fixed costs and heterogeneous preferences, trade can have subtle effects on product positioning that benefit some consumers but make others worse off. To put it another way, the availability of products targeted to consumers elsewhere (alien majorities) can help or hurt (tyrannize) consumers in the importing market.

Does this mean that trade is bad and should be restricted? Not necessarily. But it is important to understand how the "tyranny of alien majorities" argument differs from the usual argument against free trade. Restrictions on free trade are generally enacted with the goal of protecting domestic producers. For example, the U.S. textile industry has been in decline for decades. It is simply difficult for workers in South Carolina to compete with their counterparts in China. Trade protection for the domestic textile industry benefits both the firms' shareholders as well as domestic textile workers.

Discussions about trade protection are never about the range of product options available. There is no argument that once shirts are available from China (or Vietnam, South Africa, Cambodia, or Russia), U.S. consumers will no longer be able to find styles that they prefer. There is no concern that American consumers will have to forsake golf shirts and Oxford cloth for dashikis and Mao jackets. The reason there is no concern about the tyranny of alien majorities in the textile market is that shirts have trivially small fixed costs. Even if the surviving domestic firms lose half of their business, they can continue at a smaller scale as long as any consumers are willing to pay their higher prices. In addition, textile suppliers in China and scores of other countries are happy to make authentic-looking Oxford cloth and other conventional Western styles.

Not so, however, with products requiring higher fixed costs. The globalization of industries like movies, pharmaceuticals, and media products, for example, may change product options available to importers and exporters alike—improving the number and quality of choices that some consumers face, while degrading the options of others. The liberation brought about by trade in high-fixed cost goods is thus mixed.

CHAPTER 9

Salvation through New Technologies

Preference minorities face few appealing options in markets with high fixed costs relative to market size. As I have shown, one way of addressing their plight is increased market size. The other solution, of course, is to reduce the fixed costs of offering differentiated product options. While new technologies do not invariably achieve this result, technological change has been responsible for much of the improvement in our quality of life since the Industrial Revolution. Indeed, Robert Solow won a Nobel Prize in economics in part for documenting that roughly two-thirds of the increase in output per worker in the United States has been due not to growth in labor or capital in the economy but rather to growth in the amount of output produced per unit of productive input—in short, new technology as well as innovations in managerial practice.[1]

Henry Ford built Ford Motor Company into the largest automaker with the Model T, which he built to offer affordable transportation to a mass market by offering few options and using an advanced assembly line. "Beginning in 1914 and for the next eleven years, the Model T would be sold in only one color: black." Black enamel "dried more quickly than other paints and therefore sped up production."[2] As Lee Iacocca described it, Ford "basically started saying 'to hell with the customer,' who can have any color as long as it's black."[3] Ford's decision to target the low-price market led him to eschew customization, which would have increased costs.

Competition from General Motors in the 1920s eventually forced Ford to offer more variety. Since the early twentieth century, and in a variety of industries, new developments in the technologies of both information processing and production, along with innovations in managerial practice, have reduced the costs of offering products suited to more consumers' tastes. Advances in technology have improved the lot of many of the preference minorities we have encountered on our journey: the isolated radio listener and the small-town retail consumer, the 1970 television viewer, the isolated phone user, and people with rare diseases. New technologies hold the promise of liberating them still further.

Broadcast Entertainment and Communications

Think back to Chapter 1's car trip undertaken with only a car radio for entertainment. A series of technological changes have liberated the cross-country driver from this scenario of limited options. For at least twenty years it has been possible to play prerecorded music (from eight-track tapes, to cassette tapes and CDs, to today's compressed MP3s). A cross-country driver can bring thousands of his favorite songs along on his trip, fully liberating him from the radio programming made available by local demand. Satellite radio functions similarly. Hundreds of channels are available to subscribers anywhere in the satellite footprint.[4]

Similarly, until about 1980 television offered most viewers only three local options (a few more in large markets, if you count non-network stations) over public airwaves. With the advent of video distribution over cable, however, programmers began producing national channels, and by 1990 most households could purchase a cable service offering fifty channels. Today, the number of channels available on cable is two hundred, and satellite television providers offer similar numbers to any household in the United States, no matter how remote. If these hundreds of options are not enough, the Internet holds the promise of delivering video programming as well.

Traditionally, voice communication was carried over wires that had to be strung, or sunk—hence the term "sunk" cost—into trenches, to each dwelling. In dense areas, this was relatively inexpensive. In sparsely populated areas, it was expensive. Without subsidies for high-cost service, the technology would have been prohibitively expensive in remote areas. New communications technologies, including both cellular and satellite phones, change this equation considerably. A person no longer needs so many neighbors to help cover the fixed costs of serving an area.

In the previous examples, the new technology increases market size rather than reducing fixed costs. In the examples that follow, new technology and managerial innovation can reduce fixed costs.

Air Travel

Until recently commercial air travel relied on large aircraft. The aircraft in most common service have included the Boeing 737, 747, 757, and 767, as well as the Airbus A. The smallest of these aircraft, the Boeing 737–700, carries between 126 and 140 passengers and consumes the same amount of crew labor and nearly as much fuel flown empty as full.[5] As a result, carriers deploy them on routes, and at frequencies, that give rise to full aircraft.

This strategy has a few consequences. First, major air carriers have moved toward hub-and-spokes route structures, to maintain full aircraft. Too few people want to fly between Indianapolis, Indiana, and Austin, Texas, to warrant putting a 737 into service between them. But enough people will fly between Indianapolis and Chicago and between Chicago and Austin to cover the costs of these legs. So passengers tend to take one-stop flights between medium-sized cities. Second, smaller cities, such as Champaign, Illinois, received no jet service at all. A passenger traveling from Champaign had to take a propeller plane such as the nineteen-seat Beechcraft 1900 or the thirty-seven-seat DeHavilland Dash 8.

In the past few years, aircraft manufacturers such as Embraer and Canadair have begun making smaller jet aircraft, such as the fifty-seat Canadair Jet or the Embraer EMB-145. Carriers such as U.S. Airways and United have largely replaced their fleets of propeller planes and now serve cities in the population range of Lincoln, Nebraska; Fayetteville, Arkansas; or Allentown, Pennsylvania, with these "regional jets."

Smaller aircraft are a new technology that allows the use of jet service on routes formerly too small to fill, say, 737's. According to the *New York Times,* "airlines can fill up 50-seat and 70-seat regional jets on routes where they could not sell all the seats on a bigger plane."[6]

A more recent development is air taxi services, which take passengers "where you want to go when you want to go there, without changing planes along the way or making reservations three weeks in advance."[7] One company, SATSAir, uses four-seat Cirrus SR22 aircraft. SATSAir will "meet customers at any airport within its service area . . . and take up to three people directly to any destination the airplane can reach."[8] All this for $395 per hour of flight time. Another company, DayJet, plans to offer taxi service with six-passenger jets, beginning in 2006.

In air travel, then, fixed costs have been reduced by both new aircraft designs and innovative business models. Scheduled air carrier service requires both an airport and the establishment of a "station," with baggage-handling and ticket-taking facilities. Air taxi service, by contrast, requires only an adequate airport. Hence, the development of air taxis brings the market closer to the situation where an individual gets what she wants simply because she wants it. In this instance, she needs to be willing to pay $395 per hour.

Pharmaceutical Products

As noted earlier, it now costs an average of $900 million to bring a new drug to market, up from $230 million in 1987.

> The biggest expense in drug development comes not from early-stage research . . . but from the failure of drugs after they have left the labs and been tested in humans . . . To change that, [the Eli] Lilly [Company] is focusing its research effort on finding biomarkers—genes or other cellular signals that will indicate which patients are most likely to respond to a given drug . . . If all goes as planned, the company will know sooner whether its drugs are working, and will develop fewer drugs that fail in clinical trials . . . The flip side of Lilly's plan is that drugs it develops may be used more narrowly than current treatments. For example, the company may find that a diabetes drug works best in patients under 40 with a specific genetic marker, and enroll only those patients in its clinical trials.[9]

Retailing

Isolated consumers have traditionally faced modest retail options, limited by the tastes of their neighbors and overall population size. Since the appearance of the Sears catalog in 1893, isolated consumers have had access to a large number of products.[10] More recently, isolated consumers have been able to use both catalog and Internet retailers to have many nonperishable products shipped to them, even in most remote locations. The retail consumer in Fergus Falls, Minnesota, or Shelby, Montana (population 3,375), can get the same obscure books and CDs—and the same advanced electronic gadgets—as his counterparts in large metropolitan areas.

Conventional brick-and-mortar retailers have also provided some liberation to smaller-market consumers by developing smaller-format stores viable in smaller population areas. Best Buy is one example. The largest retailer of electronics in the United States, Best Buy has as its main retailing vehicle a 45,000-square-foot store. A store this large is only profitable in a large or densely populated market area, so until recently Best Buy had not penetrated smaller markets. In the past few years, however, Best Buy has introduced smaller-format stores, using 20,000 and 30,000 square feet. As the company puts it, smaller stores enable "us to reach customers in smaller markets (populations of 100,000), as well as fill in existing markets."[11]

Wal-Mart too has begun deploying a smaller-format store. Wal-Mart's dominant retail formats are its 1,353 discount stores and 1,713 supercenters. Supercenters, which encompass thirty-six general merchandise departments including groceries, average 186,000 square feet, carry over 116,000 items, and employ 350 or more associates. Wal-Mart discount stores are also large; they occupy an average of 100,000 square feet, stock 62,500 items, and employ an average of 225 people.[12] Yet since 1998 Wal-Mart has opened ninety-four "neighborhood markets," which are "40,000-square-foot facilities designed to complement and support Wal-Mart Supercenters by meeting the shopping needs of consumers who live between Supercenter locations."[13] Neighborhood markets offer about 38,000 items and employ ninety-five people. By 2005 there were eighty-five neighborhood markets. As with the smaller-format Best Buy outlets, the smaller Wal-Mart stores bring Wal-Mart to consumers in places too small to support a larger-format store.

Restaurants

Even in restaurants, whose product—hot food—does not transport nearly as well as either digital information or nonperishables, innovative business practices have reduced the fixed costs of providing another product. Offering two menus under one restaurant roof enables a business to share the kitchen and cashier costs across offerings, bringing greater variety to consumers of diverse tastes.

As we saw in Chapter 4, a restaurant requires a critical mass of customers for economic viability. Chain restaurants have traditionally offered a single firm's offerings. In the past few years, however, companies owning multiple restaurant chains have started operating multibrand restaurant outlets. For example, Yum Brands owns KFC, Taco Bell, Pizza Hut, Long John Silver's, and A&W. Almost one-sixth of the company's 18,400 U.S. stores are now multibranded.

> Yum's multibranded stores have two illuminated logos, but they function as one restaurant. They have combined kitchens, a single line of cashiers and a staff trained to prepare both sets of menu items. While Yum's multibranded restaurants are only slightly larger than individual sites in square footage, their sales are between $250,000 and $300,000 a year higher than stand-alone stores, says Mr. Deno [Dave Deno, Yum CEO] . . . According to Deno, "There are a lot of places that would be too cost-prohibitive for us to add another stand-alone KFC or Taco Bell, like high-cost urban centers or low-density rural areas . . . But as a combination, we can do it."[14]

Engineers and scientists are sometimes irritated by economists' faith that the market will provide new products as the need arises.[15] Their irritation is easy to understand: wishing—even assuming, say, that people respond to incentives—does not make things so. I have every incentive to compose music like Mozart, but I continue to compose like me. Still, economists have often been right. When the price of energy rose in the 1970s and 1980s, firms developed energy-saving technologies. When pharmaceutical firms knew that the government would compel vaccinations and pay for the indigent, the firms developed new renditions of existing vaccines. It seems safe to predict that innovations in production and distribution will continue to liberate preference minorities. But is there any predictable limit to salvation from technology?

Unfortunately, yes. First, technology reduces some kinds of fixed costs but not others. Because of the development of the computer and the Internet, the cost of producing a magazine—or better yet, a website—have become very low. For fifty dollars a month anyone can run a website competing with that of the *New York Times* or CNN. And indeed there are many websites out there (blogs in particular). Thousands of them. Does that mean that consumers are liberated? Not really. In spite of the virtually infinite number of sources of "information" on the web, the top few news sites still garner an enormous share of hits to information sites. Although new technologies make it inexpensive to post information at a site, it remains very expensive to pay reporters and editors to produce information of enough quality to attract many consumers' attention. This is powerful evidence that reductions in fixed costs do not necessarily translate into greater effective product variety. What's going on here is a variant of the story in Chapter 7 on the limits of salvation from market size.

Second, preference minorities continue to suffer with products that perforce remain local. Even with foreseeable advances in technology, some products will continue to perish in transport and will therefore remain local. Examples include fresh fish and local news. Even if it is delivered instantly, Des Moines news has the appeal of tainted oysters to most New Yorkers. As a result there is no additional nonlocal demand to be harnessed to help finance products that remain local in nature. The problem that small-market populations in general (and local preference minorities in particular) face in getting useful local news does not go away. Production of local news still requires local reporters and editors.

Today the equipment required to shoot and edit a movie, a digital camcorder and a moderately fast computer, cost just a few thousand dollars. Thus, the technological fixed costs of making a movie, like the technological fixed costs of making a magazine or a website, have fallen enormously. If that were all that mattered, then we would see a flowering of high-quality movie making. But as most people with a camcorder and a computer have realized, there's much more to movie making than technology. Just as filling a website or magazine requires the use of talented writers, a movie requires talented—and expensive—artists on both sides of the camera. Although technology has obliged, problems with variety and quality remain.

PART FOUR

POLICY SOLUTIONS
AND THEIR LIMITS

CHAPTER 10

Government Subsidies
and Insufficient Demand

What have been the policy responses to the "who benefits whom" and "tyranny of the majority" phenomena in product markets? That is, how does government address the problems of preference minorities? As emphasized earlier, there can be important shortcomings in the range of products that consumers face in markets when fixed costs are substantial. Markets can offer inefficiently too few products, or inefficiently too many. Indeed, in lumpy product markets there is no expectation that the market will generate a range of products that, like Goldilocks' porridge assessment, is "just right." Outside of efficiency concerns, there are also distributional concerns. Such markets will reward persons in large groups of well-to-do consumers with an appealing assortment of products. But regardless of an individual's buying power, if she is part of a small group of persons with atypical preferences, she will not find many appealing products. Technological advances have provided much—but not total—liberation from these features of market allocation.

With perhaps different motives in mind, policy makers (even in the generally free-market United States) have long intervened to ensure availability of products where the market, left to decide for itself, would not. Subsidies for commercial air service in small markets, development of drugs targeted at small populations, telecommunications provision in remote areas, and support of nonprofit broadcasters are but a few such initiatives. The targeting of these programs can provide clues about these policy makers' apparent intent. Are they trying to correct inefficient underprovision?

As of late 2004, conventional wired local telephone service had still not come to the fifteen households that made up the population of Mink, Louisiana.[1] More than a century after the telephone's invention, the market—with plenty of time for deliberating—had decided not to provide the community with phone service. The decision is not surprising. By one estimate, it would cost $700,000 to wire the community, or nearly $50,000 per household. A private firm could never expect to recoup this investment with revenue from the fifteen customers. If they had to rely on the market, residents of Mink would never be free to choose telephone service.

The United States has universal telephone service as a matter of policy. The only reason Mink was at the mercy of the market was a long-standing dispute over which telephone company's service area contained Mink. When the State of Louisiana ordered BellSouth to annex Mink to its territory, Mink received wired phone service. Upon hearing the news that wired phone service was coming to Mink, resident Louise Bolton, an eighty-three-year-old widow, exclaimed, "I'm so excited I can't hardly contain it."[2]

Similarly, if left to the vagaries of the market, the town of Mason City, Iowa, would have no commercial air service. A traveler interested in reaching Los Angeles would first have to drive, or ride a bus, 120 miles to Des Moines, Iowa, or 125 miles to Minneapolis, Minnesota, to board a flight to Los Angeles International Airport. Given Mason City's small population (of 28,000) and the meager volume of passengers that a carrier could expect from this market, it is not surprising that the market decided not to provide commercial air service to this community.

Since 2003, however, Mason City has received annual grants of roughly one million dollars from the U.S. Department of Transportation, allowing Mesaba Airlines to serve the community twice daily with flights to Minneapolis. Residents and political representatives of towns like Mason City, Democrats and Republicans alike, hail the subsidies. In the words of Nebraska Republican senator Chuck Hagel, "Adequate air service to rural communities is vital to their survival and to the economic well-being of the entire state."[3]

What's going on here? Why do these subsidies exist in one of the most market-oriented countries in the world? It would be no surprise to learn that France (or Sweden, or North Korea) subsidizes air service to small communities. But the United States? How widespread are such government interventions in product markets? And what do these subsidies accomplish? How and to what extent is the range of available products expanded by government intervention?

While product markets are generally thought of as private or commercial institutions, it is nevertheless true that the public sphere intervenes in many markets, and through many layers of government. Of course there is regulation, which limits the choices that sellers can make. But there are a variety of other direct interventions in markets, which fall into two categories. First, government sometimes produces a product, financing it with a mix of tax revenue and usage fees. Examples include the U.S. Postal Service and municipal public libraries. Second, various levels of government sometimes provide subsidies to firms so that their customers' revenue, in conjunction with the subsidies, allow them viability. Examples include subsidies to the nonprofit (but nongovernment) organizations that provide "public broadcasting" in the United States. Other examples that are less well known, but account for much more government expenditure, include subsidies to air transport and telecommunications firms, to induce them to serve rural and small-town customers who would otherwise not be served. These interventions are aimed squarely at expanding the availability of high fixed cost products, as opposed to enhancing the means that individuals have to buy the products available to them.

Air Transportation

In providing scheduled service to an area, air carriers must make two decisions. First, they must determine whether to serve an area at all. Serving an area requires establishing local baggage-handling, ticket-taking, and aircraft-maintenance capabilities. Second, the carrier must decide which pairs of cities its flights will connect. Because people will drive some distance to get to an airport, the geographic market supporting an airport is an entire metropolitan area and sometimes more.

Commercial aircraft come in various sizes, from the nineteen-seat Beechcraft 1900 to jumbo jets carrying hundreds of passengers, making one of the major costs of providing air service variable with the level of demand. Still, there are some fixed costs of serving a particular airport. According to the General Accounting Office, "Air service is expensive to provide, partly because of carriers' high operating costs, which are incurred whether an aircraft is flown empty or full . . . Another major part of the expense of providing air service is 'station' costs, according to airline officials. These stations require staff to handle passengers, bags, and cargo. One airline official estimated that it can cost as much as $200,000 to set up a station for new service, and annual station operating costs can range from $370,000 to $550,000."[4]

As a result of fixed costs in this industry, only relatively large metropolitan areas have scheduled commercial air service. Large metro areas, with a population greater than, say, a million, all have frequent scheduled air service. The Minneapolis–St. Paul metro area (population three million) has 783 daily direct flights to 166 different destinations. The airport in Indianapolis, Indiana, which serves an area of about 1.6 million, has 292 daily direct flights to sixty-one destinations. The Fargo, North Dakota, area, with a population of about 172,000, has twenty daily direct flights to eight destinations.[5] This is the by-now unsurprising "who benefits whom" phenomenon in high fixed cost markets: more potential travelers near an airport help each other by making more flights profitable to and from that airport.

While markets typically give consumers in larger areas choice among multiple flights and carriers, the market generally delivers fewer choices to residents of smaller towns. These are the consumers targeted by two ongoing U.S. Department of Transportation subsidies to the airline industry to encourage provision in smaller markets: the Essential Air Service (EAS) program and the Small Community Air Service Development Pilot Program (SCASDPP). Under these programs, the federal government provides funds directly to commercial air carriers that agree to serve these markets. Much larger sums are involved in the Airport Improvement Program, which provides subsidies for airport maintenance that go disproportionately to airports in small metropolitan areas.

The Essential Air Service program was established in 1978, as the U.S. airline industry was deregulated, out of a "concern that communities with relatively lower traffic levels would lose service entirely as carriers shifted their operations to larger, potentially more lucrative markets." Every community that had scheduled air service when the U.S. industry was regulated is potentially eligible for EAS support. The EAS program is designed "to ensure that smaller communities would retain a link to the national air transportation system, with Federal subsidy where necessary."[6] In 2005 the program's budget stood at $55 million.[7]

Although any community with commercial air service prior to deregulation was originally eligible for EAS subsidies, under current implementation the subsidy goes only to the larger communities that private firms would not otherwise serve. Further, "communities are not eligible to receive subsidized air service if they are within 70 driving miles of an FAA-designated Large or Medium Hub airport." This caveat rules out both subsidies for large metropolitan areas where the revenue available is sufficient to cover a carrier's costs, as well as subsidies to people near such places. Places are also ineligible "if their subsidy per passenger exceed[s] $200."[8] A typical annual route subsidy is around half a million dollars, implying that the two hundred dollar per-passenger limit rules out subsidies to places with fewer than 2,500 annual passengers. The EAS program currently subsidizes service in twenty-six Alaska communities—most of which fall under an "exception from the $200-per-passenger standard for communities that are more than 210 highway miles from the nearest" airport—along with seventy-eight communities in the rest of the United States.

The Small Community Air Service Development Pilot Program, signed into law in 2000, is "designed to help smaller communities to enhance their air service . . . The core objective of the program is to secure enhancements that will be responsive to a community's air transportation needs and whose benefits can be expected to continue after the initial expenditures . . . To be eligible for a grant, the community must [have] insufficient air carrier service; or [have] unreasonably high air fares."[9] The pilot program allocated $20 million in 2003, and it is available to communities not receiving commercial air service prior to deregulation.

Under EAS the Department of Transportation aims to serve airports with, at the smallest, nineteen-seat aircraft, and with three departures per day. With completely full aircraft, this would lead to 20,748 annual enplanements.[10] One major carrier participating in the EAS program, Great Lakes Aviation, reported average loads of about 50 percent during 2000.[11] So perhaps ten thousand is a more reasonable annual passenger load. Do we see these subsidies targeted to communities where demand for air travel would give rise to roughly ten thousand annual passengers (if service were available)? Outside of Alaska, there are 109 communities receiving subsidies through either the EAS or SCASDPP programs. The median passenger load in these communities was 5,666 (twenty-fifth percentile = 2,246, seventy-fifth percentile = 12,090). Given these passenger loads, commercial service in these areas would be barely viable; in the absence of these subsidy programs, these small markets would not have scheduled air service.

The combined budgets for these programs are a tiny fraction of the $2.5 trillion U.S. budget, but their existence betrays policy makers' concern for preference minorities, who in this case are consumers in small markets.[12]

In addition to these direct subsidies, the FAA also offers a much larger indirect subsidy to air travel through its Airport Improvement Program (AIP).[13] The 2005 federal budget allocated $3.5 billion to airport improvements. There are 3,300 U.S. airports, which are collectively thought to "provide a safe, efficient, and integrated system of airports to meet the needs of civil aviation, national defense, and the Postal service." While the majority of AIP funds go to high-volume airports, a disproportionate share of these funds go to low-volume airports, in effect providing larger subsidies to small-market travelers. For example, the top 20 percent of commercial airports handle 93 percent of passengers but receive only 30 percent of AIP funds.[14]

Among the two major political parties in the United States, the Republicans have been generally more stalwart defenders of free markets. It is perhaps surprising, then, that the Essential Air Service program, which explicitly intervenes in the market, enjoys bipartisan support. The Congressional Rural Caucus, "a bipartisan coalition of Members of Congress committed to strengthening and revitalizing rural communities across America" included seventy-eight Republicans among its 132 members during the first session of the 109th Congress.[15]

Lawmakers of both parties regard the market's failure to deliver scheduled air service to their constituents as a problem that the federal government should address. For example, Nebraska is heavily dependent on EAS subsidies for continued air service to communities outside Omaha. In 2002, Nebraska senator Chuck Hagel wrote to the Senate Transportation Appropriations Subcommittee, "This funding is critical for small communities . . . Essential Air Service greatly benefits our rural communities, and it is essential that this program receives adequate funds to keep serving our state."[16] As Nebraska Republican representative Bill Barrett explained EAS support to his state in 1995, "We're not just talking vacations here . . . This is community access, which is vital to economic viability."[17]

Broadcasting

Radio and television broadcasting, like air travel, have high fixed costs. As we have seen, because of fixed costs, larger markets bring consumers more freedom to choose among commercial radio and television programming options. Only in large metropolitan areas do markets bring forth radio stations specializing in classical music or jazz, for example.

With air travel, the key availability question is whether an area had scheduled commercial air service. For radio, by contrast, the question is not simply whether an area has service but rather what kind. Different stations offer different programming. Some broadcast country music, others rock or rap music, and still others broadcast news or talk or (rarer still) classical music or jazz.

Some programming formats are widespread even in small metropolitan areas; for example, 95 percent of the top 165 markets had at least one country music radio station in 1993. We can divide the top 165 markets into five groups ("quintiles") by population, and even among the smallest quintile of these markets, 97 percent had at least one country station.[18] Programming in some other formats is similarly widespread: Top 40, album-oriented rock, adult contemporary, news/talk, and oldies are all available in over 90 percent of the top 165 markets.

By contrast, commercial classical music and jazz, along with black- and Hispanic-targeted programming, are far less available outside the largest metropolitan areas. Outside of the top thirty metropolitan areas, only 10 percent of the remaining cities among the top 165 had a commercial classical station. Commercial jazz is only slightly more commonly available: only 10 percent of metro areas outside of the top two quintiles had one. It is quite clear that beyond the largest metropolitan areas, the market offers limited programming choices.

Nonprofit broadcasters in the United States receive subsidies from various levels of government (along with support from listeners and business underwriters) to promote the provision of radio programming, largely in news, classical music, and jazz. So-called public radio in the United States receives revenue from a mix of listeners (26 percent) business underwriters and foundations (22 percent), state and local governments (17 percent), and the federal government (19.4 percent).[19] The Corporation for Public Broadcasting (CPB) provides the bulk of the federal money (15.5 percent of public-radio funding). Total revenue to public broadcasting in 2003 was $2.3 billion, compared with revenue of $20 billion for commercial radio.[20]

The CPB seeks to "ensure universal access to non-commercial high-quality programming and telecommunications services."[21] With a $383 million budget in 2004, the CPB allocated roughly $250 million to direct grants to radio and television stations to help "local stations to provide meaningful services to their communities."[22] In so doing, the CPB helps public radio stations to operate alongside—and to some extent compete with—commercial entities.

How are the subsidies distributed? In contrast to the direct air service subsidies, which are given only to places that would receive no commercial service, CPB radio subsidies are given to a wider range of locales, including some with similar commercial programming. Yet despite these less restrictive subsidies—that is, despite the possibility for competition with private enterprises—most public radio stations offer programming in a format that would be unavailable locally in their absence. If we divide the top 165 U.S. markets into five quintiles by size, then whereas almost no markets in the bottom three quintiles have commercial classical programming, about a third have public classical stations. Only 12 percent of markets in the fourth quintile have commercial classical stations, but over half of these markets have public classical. In the largest markets, some public stations appear to compete with commercial counterparts.

What effect do public subsidies have on the range of available radio programming? The simple answer is the number of cities with classical music, say, only by a public station. But the number of cities served by public stations will generally overstate the number of additional cities served because of public stations. Why? Because the presence of, say, a public classical station makes it harder for a commercial classical station to attract listeners. And this "crowding out" is more acute as public and commercial programming are more similar.

The similarity of public and commercial programming varies across formats. Public and commercial classical music stations are close substitutes. This is evident in three ways.[23] First, even after accounting for the size of the metro area, the presence of a public classical music station depresses the probability of a commercial classical station operating nearby. Second, the presence of a public classical station reduces commercial classical listening. Finally, public and private classical stations play similar music. Mozart, Bach (including heirs), and Beethoven finished first, second, and third on both public and commercial airplay lists.

The difference between public and private programming is more pronounced in news. The presence of a public news station has no depressing effect on the number of commercial news stations operating in a metropolitan area or on commercial news listening. The effects on the market of commercial and public jazz stations fall somewhere between those of news and classical stations. The presence of a public jazz station depresses the tendency for a commercial station to offer jazz programming, but there is no discernible depressing effect of a public jazz station on commercial jazz listening.

Thus, in classical music and to a lesser extent jazz, public stations can displace commercial rivals. Absent the public stations, some cities currently served only by public stations would instead have a commercial station.

How big is this displacement effect? In the current landscape of subsidies for public stations, eighty-eight of 165 markets had either public or commercial classical programming available in 1993. If the public stations ceased to exist, then those sixty markets served exclusively by public stations would lose classical programming. In exchange, however, ten markets would gain a commercial classical station. On balance, thirty-eight (rather than eighty-eight) cities would have classical programming. Without the public stations, few stations outside the top-fifth in terms of metro population would have classical music programming on the radio.

Similarly, fifty-seven of 165 markets had jazz programming in 1993. But if the public jazz stations ceased operations, then few markets outside the top two quintiles would have jazz programming in the absence of the public jazz stations.

By contrast, given the absence of evidence that public and private news stations offer substitute programming, it seems that public news is a distinct product. Absent their public news stations, cities currently served with public news would have no similar programming.

Overall then, while public stations crowd out some private programming in classical music and jazz, for the most part public stations provide service that markets, left to themselves, would not provide.

CPB subsidies, given disproportionately to small-market public stations, are not the only government intervention in radio markets. In addition to promoting policies designed to increase service in small markets, the federal government has promoted radio programming targeted at black, Hispanic, and Native American listeners. While the First Amendment forbids direct regulation of content, until 1993 the FCC promoted targeted programming indirectly by favoring minority applicants for broadcast licenses. Of course, there is in principle no reason why minority owners would have to target minority listeners, and indeed, most minority-targeted stations are not minority-owned. Nevertheless, it is true that almost all minority owners broadcast minority-targeted programming. What's more, cities with more minority-owned stations tend to have more minority-targeted stations, even after accounting for the size of their minority populations. That is, adding minority owners adds minority-targeted programming without simply crowding out white-owned minority-targeted programming.[24]

Orphan Drugs

Ethnic minorities and small-town Americans are not the only U.S. preference minorities who benefit from government subsidies. Drugs are very expensive to develop. Because of the high cost of bringing a prescription drug to market in the United States, it is not surprising that common illnesses tend to have far more medications available than rare ones.

In 1983 the U.S. Congress passed the Orphan Drug Act, which included a number of provisions designed to stimulate the development of pharmaceutical products targeted at persons with rare conditions (that is, those that affect fewer than 200,000 persons). The provisions include grants for research aimed at the development of such drugs, and stronger patent protection for compounds receiving orphan status (competitors would not be granted any similar patents). The goal of this program, as with many other such policies, is to raise the level of satisfaction that individuals in small groups receive from product markets. Here, of course, "satisfaction" may mean survival.

Telecommunications and Electricity

Nowhere are product market subsidies larger than in telecommunications. Although traditional wired phone service is somewhat inexpensive to establish in densely populated urban areas, small-town and rural areas are a different matter. As our example of Mink, Louisiana, showed, markets on their own would not provide telephone service in sparsely populated areas. To ensure that telecommunications service is universally available, even in rural areas, the FCC administers a "High Cost" program of over $3 billion in annual subsidies for areas that would otherwise be too costly to serve. According to the Universal Service Administration, which administers these funds, "About 10% of the USA's phone lines are in rural areas, from the northern plains to the Southwest. Many are run by small family-owned phone companies and co-ops that sprang up early in the 20th century in out-of-the-way areas shunned by big carriers. Rural residents are expensive to serve. It can cost thousands to run a cable 20 miles to an isolated farmer." In response, "the High Cost support mechanism aims to meet the goal of providing consumers in all parts of the country with affordable telephone service, regardless of where they live." For example, "the Northwest Telephone Cooperative Association . . . connects over 1,000 residential and 250 business customers over a 246 square mile area and provides not only telephone service but also both dial-up and high-speed Internet access." As Don Miller, Northwest's general manager, explains, "If we did not receive Universal Service Funds . . . our customers' service and our company's future would be in jeopardy. It would create a have and have not situation in comparison with the metropolitan areas."[25]

Alaska, Wyoming, Montana, and the Dakotas are the least densely populated U.S. states, with fewer than ten people per square mile. Per-capita High Cost telecommunications subsidies in these states in 2003 ranged between $63 and $143. The most densely populated areas, like Connecticut, Massachusetts, Rhode Island, New Jersey, and the District of Columbia, have over seven hundred people per square mile. These areas receive annual subsidies of less than a dollar per person.[26]

There are similar subsidies for electricity. The U.S. Department of Agriculture's Rural Utilities Service (RUS) administers low-interest loans "to make sure that rural citizens can participate fully in the global economy."[27] The RUS provides loans and some grants for telecommunications, electricity transmission, and water treatment in rural areas. The program's goal is not simply to bring rural America to some absolute level of service quality, but also to bring rural America to parity with urban America. According to its annual report, "Some argue that the original mission of RUS has been accomplished by providing rural Americans with connections to electric, telecommunications, and water utilities. Indeed, most people in rural America receive some type of electric, telephone, and indoor running water service. However, the intent of the underlying legislation for RUS programs is not connections alone. Rather, the intent is to provide Americans—no matter where they live—the opportunity for a basic standard of living and quality of life."[28]

Financing by RUS allows people the choice of where to live—in rural or urban communities. Utilities are more expensive in rural areas, due to both the cost to build and the revenues needed to recoup that cost. Indeed, the "services financed by RUS provide the quality of life to help keep people secure where they live, work, learn, and relax." And "as telecommunications technology expands, with new and better products and services coming to urban markets, rural Americans want to be able to participate, and Federal legislation (notably the Telecommunications Act of 1996) has mandated that they be able to do so."[29]

Program goals recall the liberation rhetoric sometimes used to describe free markets. One might say that these programs aim to make rural citizens free to choose advanced telecommunications services, regardless of how many nearby consumers are available to help cover fixed costs.

The U.S. government thus intervenes in a variety of markets to promote the availability of products that consumers, because of insufficient demand, would otherwise not enjoy. The programs seem to have some effect—creating access to products that the market would not, on its own, bring forth. It is possible, moreover, that these programs actually enhance efficiency by correcting inefficient underprovision. These programs also have strong bipartisan support, stemming largely from a rural lobby, although the programs are not without detractors.

As we have seen, subsidizing provision of high fixed cost products is a fairly widespread activity. But are these programs good or bad? One perspective is that these programs are bad by definition because they entail interference with the market. But this perspective misses the point that in high fixed cost environments, markets are not necessarily efficient in contexts where revenue falls just short of costs. Suppose that the average benefit that customers experience from a product exceeds the price they pay by an average of 20 percent. Then imagine that bringing a product into existence and making enough units to meet demand (at the going price) costs $1,100. Suppose that the revenue available to the firm is only $1,000. The product's value to society is $1,200, but it does not get provided. We expect inefficient underprovision in those markets that are slightly too small for revenue to cover costs.

And in what sorts of markets do subsidies promote provision? In air travel, subsidies are unavailable to cities large enough to attract unsubsidized private entry. And they are unavailable (outside Alaska) to cities so small that the per-passenger subsidy would be enormous. In telecommunications and other utilities, there is a commitment to universal service, which entails serving customers so isolated—like those in Mink, Louisiana—that their provision may not provide benefits in excess of costs. Further, although it may be true that concerns of "fairness" rather than efficiency drove the development of these programs, given that the free market outcome is not efficient, these interventions may in fact enhance efficiency.

CHAPTER 11

Books and Liquor:
Two Case Studies

Most people do not realize that the stamp they use to send their letters represents a dramatically egalitarian way of treating customers. The U.S. Postal Service, the only entity legally authorized to deliver letters to mailboxes, charges the same rates regardless of distance or destination within the United States.

Suppose I want to send letters to West Philadelphia (zip code 19104) from two locations: Shelby, Montana (zip code 59474), and the University of Chicago (zip code 60637). Chicago is a large metropolitan area served by frequent flights and two major interstate highways, whereas Shelby, Montana, is quite remote. With a population of 3,216 in 2000, Shelby sits near the Canadian border, in the western third of the state. The nearest population center is eighty-five miles away in Great Falls, Montana (population 55,000). Private shippers, such as United Parcel Service (UPS), charge different rates to send packages to and from Shelby than to and from Chicago. To send a package to Philadelphia from the two locations, for example, UPS Second Day Air (as of 2005) is $14.51 from Chicago and $18.51 from Shelby; Next Day Air (by the end of the day) is $18.61 from Chicago and $28.08 from Shelby. Two quicker UPS service options, both for delivery the morning of the next day, are not even available for Shelby, although they are offered for Chicago.[1] These variations in prices and service reflect the different costs of serving these destinations.

If we relied on markets to determine the availability of service options, consumers in Shelby would face less appealing options—in this case higher prices and fewer shipping choices—than their counterparts in Chicago. But U.S. policy does not "let the market decide" what prices and product options will be available in Shelby and Chicago. Instead, the U.S. government operates the U.S. Postal Service, which charges the same amount to mail the letter to any location in the United States. As of 2005, first-class mail, estimated to take three days, is $0.37, Priority Mail, estimated to arrive in two days, is $3.85, and Express Mail, which ships overnight to most areas (although not Shelby, Montana) is $13.65.[2] Uniform postal pricing gives consumers the same level of satisfaction from letter-delivery service regardless of their decisions about where to live.

Commercial goods and services, along with market mail service, are also sparse in Shelby. The town has only twenty-five retail establishments, and no bookstore. (The nearest bookstore is in Great Falls.) Yet Shelby does benefit from a government-subsidized library. The town is home to the Toole County Public Library with 22,000 volumes and an annual budget of $70,000. Annual library attendance is 11,000, and annual circulation is nearly 22,000 volumes (roughly half of which involves children's books).

In fact, libraries serve many areas that are underserved by bookstores. Zip code 19132 in West Philadelphia, for example, with a population of 35,000, has a median household income of $18,961, less than half the national average of $39,728.[3] Commercial services generally are available but not plentiful in the area: just two per thousand residents (a nearby affluent suburb has five per thousand residents). While nearly 70 percent of U.S. zip codes with populations similar to West Philadelphia's 19132 (between 34,000 and 36,000) contain a bookstore, 19132 does not. Yet, zip code 19132 has a public library.

When we rely on government rather than markets for delivery of a good or service, are the outcomes different? These anecdotes suggest that the government serves poor and sparsely populated areas that markets avoid. Is there systematic evidence for this suggestion?

When economists compare government provision to markets, they typically focus on how privatization can lower costs.[4] Cost reduction is not the only important issue, however. While markets can provide many goods, it remains unclear whether market provision will be efficient when the assumptions of the perfectly competitive model do not hold (for example, when there are substantial fixed costs). That a market can provide a good does not demonstrate the superiority of market provision over alternative arrangements. What we want to know is how government and market provision compare for some real-world markets. What products are made available? Who gets served? How do preference minorities fare?

Finding apples-to-apples comparisons of market and government provision is inherently difficult. An ideal answer to this question requires parallel universes, identical except for whether private firms or government entities provide the product in question. This chapter provides perhaps the next best thing: two comparisons that share some important features of ideal examples, libraries versus bookstores and municipal versus private liquor stores. For historical reasons, U.S. municipalities operate public libraries alongside a private book-selling industry. Roughly 12,000 bookstores sell books alongside about 17,000 municipal libraries that lend books, and to a lesser extent videos and music, without charge. Retail distribution of liquor is done by private firms in most places. But some states, and some towns, run government liquor stores and forbid private firms selling liquor within their borders. These examples allow a nearly controlled comparison of government and markets.

If the retail provision of books or liquor is subject to high fixed costs relative to market size—if book and liquor stores will be few and far between—where will they locate? And which sorts of consumers—black or white, small-town or big-city—win or lose from government provision?

Product Availability under Markets and Government

With high fixed costs, what sort of product provision do we expect from markets as opposed to government? Private firms enter if they expect revenues in excess of their costs. Given a level of fixed costs, the key determinant is revenue, which in turn depends on the number of potential consumers and their means. The larger the market—the more potential consumers with a given level of means—the more products (or outlets) will be available.

When there is a low level of demand in a place with few potential buyers, revenue cannot cover costs, and no businesses will answer the needs or wishes of the hopeful consumers. Regardless of how badly individuals want the product, or desire a nearby place to buy it (or "outlet"), unless enough other nearby people also do, it will not be provided. As demand crosses a threshold, however, an outlet can be profitable and will open for business. Eventually, as demand rises, two competing outlets can be profitable. If the existence of a second firm nearby places downward pressure on prices, then locations will require more than double the number of potential customers to support two outlets than are needed to support one. Additional demand may support even more outlets, provided that prices are not driven too low for profitability.[5]

As noted, when fixed costs are substantial, markets can "get it wrong" in two ways. First, there can be levels of demand sufficient that the social benefit of a first firm's entry exceeds cost but the revenue available does not cover costs. That is, if the firm cannot capture all the social benefit as revenue, there can be inefficient underprovision at low-to-intermediate levels of demand. At the same time, there can be situations with high demand where the revenue available covers the costs of multiple firms' outlets, even when the cost of an additional outlet exceeds its social benefit. In other words, at high levels of demand, there can be inefficient over-provision in markets.

How might government support or subsidy change this situation? Let's look at our library example. A private bookstore chooses a location where it can get revenue in excess of costs. A municipal library, however, has different goals. First, library location and staffing decisions are made through political processes—that is, libraries need not seek revenue from their users. As a result, the goals of library managers can diverge from private managers' goals. For example, the Friends of the Free Library of Philadelphia "believe that every neighborhood in every city, rich or poor, deserves equal access to the educational services provided at libraries."[6]

Municipal and Market Book Distribution

Both theoretical considerations, and over $10 billion in annual U.S. bookstore revenue, attest to the fact that books can be provided through markets.[7] For historical reasons, though, there is a public book distribution system—the public library—operating parallel to the book retailing industry. Ben Franklin helped establish the Library Company in Philadelphia in 1731.[8] The Boston Public Library, established in 1848, was the first large free municipal public library in the United States.[9] And between 1889 and 1923, Andrew Carnegie funded 1,681 library buildings, with "a great impact on the growth of the public library movement in the United States."[10]

The library and bookstore sectors are of roughly comparable size. In 1997 there were 17,041 public library locations in the United States employing 121,000 persons. Total government expenditure on libraries was nearly $6 billion. (Of this, over 75 percent was financed locally, 12 percent by states, and under 1 percent by the federal government.) Library attendance was just over one billion visits (not patrons), and 1.69 billion items circulated during the year, most of them books (94.5 percent of libraries' collections are books). Libraries spent $891 million on their collections in 1997. Similarly, in 1997 there were 12,372 bookstores in the United States, employing 121,000 persons, and generating an overall revenue of over $12 billion; the publishing industry in general garnered $17.2 billion in revenue.[11]

Library and Bookstore Availability

In order to analyze in a simple way what determines bookstore and library availability, it is first necessary (as with the study of restaurants in Chapter 4) to determine the relevant market area. We need to ask, "What is the smallest geographic area for which local supply serves local demand?" The right level of geography is not obvious a priori, although introspection helps a bit. For example, it is certainly true that the vast majority of a bookstore's customers are from its home metropolitan area. Consequently, metro area demand is the relevant determinant of metro area supply. At the same time, because there are multiple locations of a bookstore chain in a large metro area, the market area is presumably much smaller than the large metro area.[12] There are twenty Borders locations, and sixteen Barnes & Noble stores, within twenty-five miles of the West Philadelphia zip code 19104. Hence, the relevant market area is much smaller than a metro area.

Our strategy to find a geographic area suitable for analysis is to relate supply, measured by the number of available bookstores, to demand (measured by population) at successively smaller geographic areas. To this end, we could relate the number of bookstores operating to the population at the three-digit and five-digit zip code levels. Across the 894 three-digit zip codes, which average 344,000 in population and contain an average of nineteen libraries, an additional thousand residents adds 0.02 libraries. Three-digit zip codes contain an average of fourteen libraries, and an additional thousand people add 0.04 bookstores. At the finer level of dis-aggregation of five-digit zip codes, the relationships are nearly identical. This suggests that, as with restaurants, the five-digit zip code is a reasonable market area.

Population and Book Availability

Places with more residents have more bookstores and more libraries. We can divide the roughly thirty thousand U.S. zip codes into ten groups, or "deciles," by population. Figure 4 shows the share of zip codes in each population decile in which bookstores and libraries are present. Zip codes with more people have more bookstores and more libraries, but there are interesting differences between the patterns for bookstores and libraries. The bottom 60 percent of zip codes by population are quite unlikely to have a bookstore, only about 10 percent of zip codes in the seventh population decile have a bookstore, and then bookstore presence rises rapidly to nearly 70 percent in the top population decile. Municipal libraries, by contrast, achieve that 10 percent level of prevalence in the second population decile. Library presence rises steadily across deciles until the seventh, when it generally levels off at about 70 percent. Figure 5 repeats the exercise for the number of outlets rather than whether an outlet is available. The relationships are similar, although more pronounced. Bookstores are actually more numerous than libraries, per zip code, in the top two population deciles.

What do these relationships mean? For the 82 million people in the bottom 80 percent of zip codes (by population)—like the people of Shelby, Montana—the nearest source of books is more likely to be a library rather than a bookstore. Residents of the most populous 20 percent of zip codes (which contain 71 percent of U.S. population), meanwhile, are more likely to be nearer to a bookstore than a library.

As in other contexts, we find here that individuals in places where

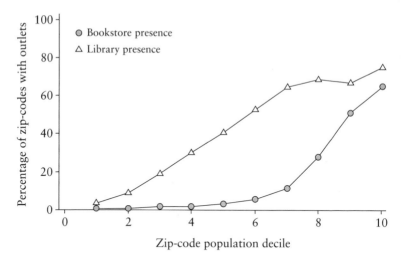

FIGURE 4. Bookstore and library presence by zip-code population. The figure shows the relationship between the size of a zip code—measured by population—and the probability that the zip code contains bookstores and libraries. To this end, zip codes are grouped into ten population deciles for calculating the share of zip codes in each decile containing a bookstore or a library.

demand is sparse face fewer product options. This is acutely true with bookstores, whose presence in an area is more likely than not only in areas that are in the ninth population decile (where the zip code population averages 21,000) or above. The probability of having a library nearby, however, crosses 50 percent in the sixth population decile, where the zip code population averages 3,300. Thus, the public sphere provides greater access to books to persons who live in sparsely populated places.

This example offers evidence of both under- and overprovision of market-based supply in various contexts, as the theoretical models suggest. As explained earlier regarding underprovision, unless sellers can perfectly customize prices to extract consumers' willingness

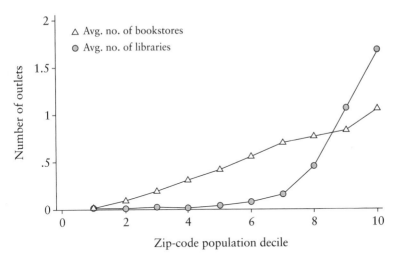

FIGURE 5. Numbers of bookstores and libraries by zip-code population. The figure shows the relationship between the size of a zip code—measured by population—and the number of bookstores and libraries that the zip code contains. To this end, zip codes are grouped into ten population deciles for calculating the average numbers of bookstores and libraries in each zip code.

to pay, sometimes revenue will fall short of the full social benefit of providing a product, so that even though the benefit would justify providing it, there will be insufficient revenue to cover costs. It is easy to imagine, although hard to verify, that the low-population zip codes exemplify this phenomenon.

As for overprovision of a product through market processes, at the highest levels of population, most zip codes have more than one bookstore. Multiple bookstores in a small area can, of course, benefit consumers through variety, price competition, and extreme proximity. But operating bookstores entails fixed costs such as building leases and some part of labor costs; consequently multiple nearby bookstores may constitute inefficiently excessive entry.

Commercial and Public Liquor Distribution

Most towns in Minnesota rely exclusively on the market for the retail distribution of liquor, but 230 Minnesota towns, ranging in size from the tiny hamlet of Elizabeth (with a year 2000 city population of 172 within a township population of 722) to large urbanized areas such as the wealthy Minneapolis suburb of Edina (with a year 2000 city population of 47,425), distribute liquor exclusively through municipally owned stores. What effect does municipal involvement have on the availability of a nearby liquor store? Does it bring about greater availability in sparsely populated areas? Or in denser areas?

As it turns out, municipal provision appears to have two effects: it makes availability substantially more likely in small places, and it limits the number of stores in places of high demand.

To see the effect of the decision to have municipal stores, we first need to know what the market would have delivered. For a sense of this effect, we can take a look across market-reliant areas of different size, asking how many stores have been opened by private firms. Of those towns with fewer than a thousand persons that rely on the market for liquor retailing, just one-quarter have a store. Of the market towns with between one thousand and five thousand inhabitants, 63 percent have a store. And nearly all (95 percent) of the towns with populations of over five thousand that rely on the market have at least one store. The biggest determinant of whether there are private stores in town is population.

Eighty towns of fewer than a thousand residents have a municipal liquor store. Absent their municipal stores, only a quarter of these towns would have had a local store, if these towns are similar to small towns relying on private provision. Thus these towns' decision to operate municipal stores increased the probability of provision by roughly 75 percent. For towns with populations between one thousand and five thousand, the alternative to municipal provision is a 37 percent chance of having no liquor stores.

At higher levels of population, municipal provision has a different effect. Virtually all of the towns with more than ten thousand residents have liquor stores even in the absence of municipal involvement. Indeed, the towns without municipal stores average 6.3 stores per town. The towns with municipal stores, by contrast, average 2.5 stores. That is, in comparatively large areas, the market brings forth more stores than does government. (This comparison overstates somewhat because the market-only towns are larger on average. If we statistically control for town population, then even among the towns with populations over ten thousand, the private-only towns have three more stores than do the municipal-liquor-store towns.)

The private-public comparison reveals similar patterns in both Minnesota liquor retailing and the bookstore-library example. In both cases, government provision raises the availability for individuals in low-demand areas and reduces availability of multiple outlets in high-demand areas.

Municipal liquor stores spark some controversy. During 2005 a Minnesota Republican lawmaker introduced legislation to end municipal involvement in liquor retailing, arguing that "directly competing with private companies is wrong . . . Minnesota law allows local governments, using taxpayer dollars, to own and operate liquor stores in competition with private business owners—that just doesn't make sense." He continued, "But if that's not bad enough, Minnesota also allows cities to create a liquor store monopoly."[13] And the Minnesota state auditor, in her annual report on the state's municipal stores, wrote, "There is no real reason for a municipality to have a liquor store unless it is making money that can be used for local government activities that would otherwise have to be paid for with increased property taxes."[14]

If the number of stores were the same, regardless of whether a town had market or government provision—that is, if municipalities simply aped the market—then the use of the tools of government for provision would have no effect on consumers' options. But what we see, instead, is a rather different pattern of provision under government. Small municipalities provide stores where markets would not. And in larger municipalities, where markets would provide stores, municipalities provide fewer. Although larger places could support market stores, in very small places, reliance on markets would leave residents without nearby access to liquor.

This is perhaps not surprising in light of the profitability of stores in smaller places. The ratio of net income to sales averages nearly 8 percent in municipal stores in places with more than five thousand residents. In places with one thousand to five thousand residents, however, municipal stores are somewhat less profitable—the ratio of net income to sales is 7 percent. And in places with populations smaller than one thousand, which have disproportionate numbers of municipal liquor stores, the stores' average ratio of net income to sales is lower still (the median is 5 percent). Thus, the government is providing stores in places where low profitability limits the number of commercial outlets.

Race and the Availability of Bookstores and Libraries

In general, the larger the population, the more likely that both markets and governments will reward that population with books (through bookstores or libraries) and liquor (via market- or municipal-based stores). But do markets and governments reward all sorts of people—blacks and whites, rich and poor—equally? Among places of the same overall population, does a heavily black area have more or fewer bookstores and/or libraries than does a heavily white area? How about libraries?

In *Capitalism and Freedom,* Milton Friedman argues that free-market capitalism ensures the greatest freedom for all citizens. He singles out ethnic minorities:

> The groups in our society that have the most at stake in the preservation and strengthening of competitive capitalism are those minority groups which can most easily become the object of distrust and enmity of the majority—the Negroes, the Jews, the foreign-born, to mention the most obvious. Yet, paradoxically enough, the enemies of the free market—the Socialists and Communists—have been recruited in disproportionate measure from these groups. Instead of recognizing that the existence of the market has protected them from the attitudes of their fellow countrymen, they mistakenly attribute the residual discrimination to the market. (p. 21)

The evidence on race and product availability provides a test of Friedman's assertion. If access to products is the freedom that product markets create, then we can ask—based on evidence for one product category—whether markets or government bring greater freedom to minorities.

How does the availability of bookstores—and libraries—vary with black and white population? As we saw earlier, places with little population overall have few bookstores. As the population rises, the number of bookstores increases as well—but it increases more quickly with a rise in the white population than with a rise in the black population. Indeed, bookstore availability is roughly three times more sensitive to the population of whites than to the population of blacks.

How about libraries? As we saw earlier, even places with very few residents are likely to have a library. Library availability grows with both white and black population, and at about the same rate, though it is slightly more sensitive to black than white population.

It would be natural to assume that under commercial-free entry, sellers would go where the buyers are, and that income levels would be an important part of determining where the most likely buyers are located. Significantly, in the United States income levels vary by race. Mean per capita income in the United States in 2000 was $21,865 for whites and only $14,803 for blacks. According to the Consumer Expenditure Survey, conducted for the U.S. Census by the Bureau of Labor Statistics, white households spend an average of $136 on reading materials per year, compared with $53 for blacks. At least part of this difference is attributable to different income levels. While households with incomes greater than $70,000 spend an average of $243 per year on reading materials, those with incomes between $20,000 and $30,000 spend $95. Because whites far outnumber blacks (by about eleven to three), aggregate white income (computed by weighting population by per capita income) exceeds aggregate black income by even more.

Indeed, if we relate bookstore availability to aggregate black and white income in a zip code, black and white dollars (as opposed to black and white population) carry roughly the same weight in determining bookstore availability. That is, an additional million dollars of local aggregate black income has about the same effect on bookstore availability as an additional million dollars of white income. But it takes more black than white households to get to a million dollars of aggregate revenue—which may well explain why bookstore availability is so much more sensitive to increases in white population than increases in black population. Commercial firms go where the money is, and whites have more money.

Why does a black person of a particular income level encounter fewer bookstores? Because black people typically live among other black people. And because blacks tend to have less income than whites, regardless of a particular person's spending power, if his neighbors do not spend as much on the product, then the black citizen will require more black neighbors to make a retail outlet viable than a white citizen—with white neighbors—would require. In markets with fixed costs, my neighbors limit the extent to which I am "free to choose."

It is in fact true that black neighborhoods do not have a lot of bookstores. But as we saw in Chapter 4, blacks can cluster together in neighborhoods to get appealing restaurants. Why not bookstores too?

The answer to the question has two parts. First, bookstores and libraries have much larger fixed costs than restaurants. In 1997 the number of libraries and bookstores together totaled 30,000, compared with roughly 500,000 restaurants. It takes more population to support a bookstore than a restaurant.[15]

Second, because black people in general have more limited means than white people, their goals in choosing a particular area in which to live may not all be fulfilled. That is, given that neighborhood choice already depends on finding a good match for schools and housing, there may not be enough neighborhoods (in a metropolitan area) for people to simultaneously accomplish all of their material objectives, including close access to a bookstore. The problem has no obvious solution, but it is a feature of how markets deliver the satisfactions of high fixed cost products to people of diverse preferences.

In sum, for books and liquor, allocation through markets, as opposed to through government institutions, provides less access to persons in sparsely populated areas and more access in places with large populations. For books, allocation through markets provides more access to whites than blacks, while allocation through the government rewards blacks roughly the same as it rewards whites.

Two points are important to make here. First, the decision to allocate through government changes who the winners are. Second, given that these contexts—books and liquor distribution—feature substantial fixed costs relative to market size, there was no reason to expect the market allocation to have been efficient. In fact, we would have expected inefficient underprovision in small markets and inefficient overprovision in places offering high demand. What we see is that government allocation raises the availability of products like books and liquor for small populations and attenuates it for large populations. Given that the market solution had no claim of being optimal, there is no reason to believe that government allocation is worse; indeed, there is some reason to think that it is more efficient than the market outcome.

Conclusion

What have we learned in our tour of various industries, fixed costs, market enlargement, and policy interventions?

There are four basic lessons, and the first is theoretical: When markets are lumpy—when fixed costs are substantial—there is no theoretical reason to expect market outcomes to be efficient. While it is true that in a perfectly competitive market, everything that should be done will be done and nothing that should not be done will, this expectation does not carry over to realistic, high-fixed-cost examples. The point is that in an industry whose production technology gives rise to lumpy outcomes, the market solution has no claim to optimality. For people inclined to favor markets because of their efficiency properties, many real-world industries lack an efficiency rationale for a hands-off—or "laissez-faire"—approach.

Second, many markets are in fact lumpy. We saw this in local media markets. But we also saw it in restaurants, retailing, movies, pharmaceutical products, air travel, and a host of other realms. The lumpiness means that markets do not generally make available a full range of products. Instead, markets bring forth products desired by large concentrations of people. This manifests itself in two ways: (1) the "who benefits whom" phenomenon, in which people are better off, in their capacity as product consumers, if more fellow consumers share their product preferences, and (2) the tyranny of the majority in product markets. In the extreme, when there is only one product, and when its features can be tailored to please one group or another, the product is targeted to the larger group, making members of the large group better off and others worse off. In other words, markets do not avoid the problems inherent in collective choice.

Third, various forces that raise market size in relation to fixed costs—including trade across geography, managerial innovation, and technological change that allows a product to be viable with a local following—liberate isolated consumers. Indeed, consumers of many products, such as television, automobiles, drugs, and air travel, have experienced substantial product market liberation. But the extent of liberation from trade is limited by factors that keep fixed costs high even relative to enlarged market size, as in movies, newspapers, and magazines.

Fourth, government does intervene in product markets, both with subsidies to private firms (as in air travel, telecommunications, drugs, and broadcasting) and through government provision directly (as in book and liquor distribution). When distribution takes place through government, rather than the market, then different consumers benefit. Markets reward large and rich groups with product availability. Government provision rewards consumers in sparsely populated areas, as well as consumers of more limited means.

The main point is that the way markets work entails shortcomings akin to the shortcomings of voting. Markets do not avoid the tyranny of the majority. While this finding may motivate policy makers to intervene in markets more liberally, this lesson also has implications for how economists think about a variety of phenomena, including—but by no means limited to—trade, urban economics, and antitrust.

Trade

Economists of all stripes embrace free trade. Trade is thought to liberate consumers. But when fixed costs are large, trade does not merely increase the number of options available to consumers. Instead, by causing a repositioning of domestic options, opening up trade can change the kinds of options available. Rather than benefiting all consumers, then, trade can benefit some consumers while harming others. (This argument is entirely distinct from the conventional argument that trade harms some producers.) A likely fruitful area of further research, then, is the changes in options brought about by trade.

Urban Economics

The "who benefits whom" phenomenon benefits consumers who participate in markets with other buyers who share their preferences. For products that are local, the benefit accrues to people who live in the same geographic area as others with similar preferences. We saw this in local media products, where consumers gain from residing in the same metropolitan area. And we saw it with products that are even more local, such as restaurants and churches or synagogues, where consumers benefit from living in the same neighborhood as others with similar preferences.

The question of why cities exist has occupied much scholarly attention. Chapters 3 and 4 provide evidence on a little-studied aspect—the consumption benefits of agglomeration. One of the benefits of living among many people, particularly many people who share our preferences, is access to the high fixed cost products that we find appealing.

Residential segregation is also an ongoing concern of policy makers and scholars. U.S. cities are highly segregated by race and by Hispanic status.[1] The persistence of segregation even as direct obstacles to residential mobility have eroded has been something of a puzzle. But the "who benefits whom" phenomenon in product markets may provide one contributing explanation for continued, voluntary segregation. Lumpy product markets benefit consumers who reside among others sharing their preferences. An orthodox Jew moving far outside a neighborhood enclave of orthodox Jews will have to travel prohibitively far to temple and will also, in most neighborhoods, have trouble finding kosher groceries and prepared food, not to mention other specialized products. The same is true for any group with distinct preferences for high fixed cost local goods.

Antitrust

Since the late 1970s, when various industries like airlines and trucking were deregulated, antitrust enforcement has remained one of the major remaining forms of industrial regulation.[2] Broadly, antitrust enforcement seeks to protect consumers from high prices. To this end, certain kinds of conduct by firms—for example, price fixing and collusive agreement on output levels—are proscribed under U.S. law. Mergers that would threaten to substantially increase prices are also regulated and generally forbidden.[3]

A focus on prices is entirely understandable in a world of homogeneous products. With many firms, the market is perfectly competitive, and prices fall toward marginal costs. As the number of firms declines, say because of higher fixed costs, the market becomes oligopolistic and, in the extreme, with only one firm, monopolistic. Consequently, prices rise. Higher prices harm consumers in obvious ways. Some of this harm is offset because consumers' losses are gained by producers. But high prices also prevent some transactions that should take place: in particular, those that occur when consumers' valuations exceed the cost of producing another unit but fall short of the price that a seller requires.

When products are differentiated, as in most of the examples here, then mergers may affect outcomes of interest differently. First, here too the increased ownership concentration could cause prices to rise. Products can be more or less similar. If the merging products are very similar—both are, say, "branded cola beverages"—then we would expect the prices to increase substantially. But prices are not the only outcomes that might be affected by merger, given that the merging firms' products are not identical. Following a merger, a single owner controls the targeting of both products. To the extent that the products "steal business" from one another—compete for the same customers—the new joint owner is engaged in wasteful competition with himself. The merged entity might do better by making the products more distinct, thus boosting product variety.

Effects like these have been documented following mergers in various differentiated products industries. The experience of the radio broadcast industry following the 1996 Telecommunications Act provides some evidence regarding the possible effects of mergers on product variety.[4] Prior to the act, a firm could own no more than two stations in a metropolitan area. Following it, a firm could own as many as eight stations in the largest markets. Within a few years after the act's passage, concentration of ownership had increased substantially. By 1997 the number of distinct owners per market had declined by about a quarter. And as one might expect, the merged entities positioned their products differently. In markets experiencing greater growth in ownership concentration, there was a greater increase in the number of programming formats. As predicted, increased concentration led firms to reduce the amount of programming duplication across jointly owned stations in the same city. Systematic analysis of the newspaper industry finds that those metro areas with more growth in ownership concentration over time also experienced a distancing of their products—that is, their products had less similar coverage.[5]

While this is an area of economics where more research is needed, this much is clear: theory, as well as existing studies, indicate that mergers affect the positioning of differentiated products as well as their prices. Both of these outcomes affect the satisfaction that consumers experience from product markets. Just as the control of prices is a legitimate (and existing) goal of antitrust regulation, the use of regulation to beneficially influence the range of available products may be important as well. As we learn more, we may find that while mergers raise prices, they also affect product positioning in ways that, in turn, affect different consumers differently.

So, overall, do shortcomings of market allocation warrant government intervention? Markets alone are an attractive way of organizing economic activity because, without government intervention, they are supposed to be efficient in bringing forth products that ought to be provided. This is the efficiency-based argument for free-market capitalism. And, of course, this is true in the "smooth" version of our example without setup costs. But with fixed costs, markets on their own can give rise to too many or too few products and firms. Some people get served; others do not. The proposition that laissez-faire brings about optimality is thus no longer available to argue against regulation.

But even absent the argument that market outcomes are by their nature efficient, there remains an important argument favoring laissez-faire. It is that market outcomes, while imperfect, are nevertheless less imperfect than the outcomes that ensue with government intervention. This argument, in turn, has two variants, "stupid government" and "evil government."

The first—"stupid government"—is that government is clumsy, employing one-size-fits-all approaches that are inefficient in a world of varied citizens and consumers.[6] One type of stupid government maneuver is high cost provision. There is evidence that when activities are privatized, they are done at a lower cost than when done by government.

Critics of government often point to money-losing government enterprises as evidence of stupid government. According to this view, government enterprises should be businesslike in their function. Like private firms, they should seek to make profits, or at least to cover their costs, through prices or "user fees." Those government enterprises that lose money would then be deemed failures that should be shut down. This view seems to miss many of the points advanced in this book. The reason for resorting to government is that something worth doing is not being done in a market. And the only reason that private firms would not undertake something worth doing is that the revenue available to the activity falls short of costs, even though the social benefit exceeds costs. In that situation, a private firm could not be profitable. Nor could a government agency aping a private firm. Profitability would thus be the wrong criterion for judging government provision.

The other variant of the case against using government—"evil government"—is that government is simply a means by which politicians steal from people, to line their own pockets or possibly the pockets of low-income majorities.[7] There is ample evidence that government corruption in developing countries today—and in the United States in earlier times—inhibited growth and efficiency. A variant on corruption is regulatory capture, in which an agency that is set up to regulate an industry for social benefit ends up regulating the industry for the benefit of the industry. Widely cited examples include the U.S. Civil Aeronautics Board and the Interstate Commerce Commission prior to their dissolutions.

The possible shortcomings of government may indeed give cause to prefer less-than-perfectly efficient markets over interventionist alternatives that are even worse. But the theoretical superiority of "smart," perfectly competitive markets over either of the pathological forms of government hardly shows the superiority of markets over government intervention in all circumstances.

We live in an era of almost limitless faith in markets and almost limitless scorn for government. These views are held by those at the highest levels of the U.S. government. In his remarks at a ceremony honoring Milton Friedman's ninetieth birthday, President George W. Bush paid tribute to Friedman's "vision of a society where men and women are free, free to choose, but where government is not as free to override their decisions." Bush continued, "Milton Friedman has shown us that when government attempts to substitute its own judgments for the judgments of free people, the results are usually disastrous. In contrast to the free market's invisible hand, which improves the lives of people, the government's invisible foot tramples on people's hopes and destroys their dreams."[8]

Theoretical efficiency properties alone do not generally tell us whether to favor unregulated markets. The correct balance between free markets and intervention depends on the magnitude of the shortcomings of the market, in relation to the shortcomings of government interventions, for the specific industry in question. In short, there are no pat answers. But a society needs to discuss the shortcomings of market allocation honestly—and with evidence—when choosing whether to let the market decide. By presenting evidence in this book on how some real-world markets function, I hope to stimulate a more balanced discourse on public policy in this area.

NOTES

REFERENCES

CREDITS

INDEX

Notes

Introduction

1. See "The Black Population in the United States: March 2002" and "The Hispanic Population in the United States: March 2002," www.census.gov (accessed 10/3/06).

1. Markets and the Tyranny of the Majority

1. Indeed, it is fairly difficult to come up with many products that are homogeneous, although examples arguably include steel, petroleum, wheat, and shares of a particular firm's stock. As consumer products, many of these are ultimately differentiated by location: for example, gasoline at a station near my house is not the same product as gasoline available across town in that I must travel to obtain the cross-town fuel.
2. This characterization of differentiation originates with Hotelling (1929).
3. From red to violet by way of orange, yellow, green, and blue. See "Color Wavelength," www.usbyte.com (accessed 6/9/04).
4. In the economic literature on these sorts of models, pricing is a central question, and I do not deny its importance. I abstract away from pricing here for two reasons. First, my interest is in product positioning and availability rather than prices. Second, the analytics needed to discuss pricing put the arguments outside the reach of a general reader. See Hotelling (1929), d'Aspremont, Jaskold-Gabszewicz, and Thisse (1979), and Economides (1989, 1993).
5. To see this, find the distance along the color spectrum x such that x

times the number of customers per unit length (100 blacks divided by 20 units, or 5) equals the setup costs of $100. Because there are five customers per unit interval, black-targeted varieties locate no closer than 4 units from one another (100/(5 * 5) = 4). Mildly complicated things happen near 0 and 20, which I ignore because they don't change the basic story.

6. If we maintain the assumptions that prices are constant and that all consumers buy, then there is really no interesting decision for sellers to make. Regardless of where the single product locates, it will attract all consumers and will cover its costs. This scenario is unrealistic because in real life people have the option of not consuming. For example, as we see later, only about half of households purchase a daily newspaper. There is some location that will minimize the distance to customers—and therefore maximize satisfaction—but there is no reason why the firm would prefer one location over another if—again—by assumption, all persons purchase.

2. Are "Lumpy" Markets a Problem?

1. It is outside the scope of this book to discuss that work in any detail, but the interested reader is directed to Becker (1971) for a classic treatment or Ayres (2001) for a recent summary of novel approaches to measurement.

2. See, for example, "Prevalence and Incidence of Peanut Allergies," www.wrongdiagnosis.com (accessed 6/11/04).

3. One can infer that there are low fixed costs from the large number of products on the market.

4. These theoretical arguments are set out in Spence (1976a, 1976b), as well as Dixit and Stiglitz (1977). Heal (1980) makes similar theoretical arguments.

5. The arguments here are made technically by Spence (1976a, 1976b), Heal (1980), and Mankiw and Whinston (1986). Berry and Waldfogel (1999a) provide evidence that markets bring forth excessive entry, for the production of advertising, in radio broadcasting.

6. Even the libertarian thinkers at the Cato Institute agree that the federal government should provide national defense.

7. There are interesting debates over whether, and which, externalities require government intervention. Suppose that instead of polluting air,

the factory polluted water in a privately owned stream. Then the owner of the stream could charge me for the water I pollute, making the cost of water use part of the cost of the product. The product's price would then reflect its full cost of production, and people would not consume too much. When an externality involves small numbers of "injurers" and "victims," one of whom owns the resource in question, they can find a way to get the cost of the resource damage incorporated into the market solution. But when many parties are involved and/or no one "owns" the resource—think of air, breathed by many, owned by none—then such bargaining is impossible. See Coase (1960).

8. These ideas were introduced by Akerlof (1970) and have been developed extensively by A. Michael Spence and Joseph Stiglitz, who shared a Nobel Prize with Akerlof for this body of work.

9. See Friedman (1962), p. 120.

10. See ibid. Friedman goes on, however, to note that "the issues raised by monopoly are technical and cover a field in which I have no special competence."

11. See Rabin (1993) or Fehr and Schmidt (1999) for developments of these ideas.

12. The empirical study first documenting this anomalous concern for fairness is Guth, Schmittberger, and Schwarze (1982).

13. See Wolf (1988).

14. There are some circumstances when voting can yield efficient results. Suppose a society is trying to decide how much of some collective (socially shared) good to have—for example, how many dams, or how many missile shields. Each person has a most-preferred number and prefers other quantities, either more or fewer. The efficient amount for society to provide is the mean, or average, of each person's ideal amount. What will voting give? Imagine two teams trying to win voter support with proposals of different numbers of, say, dams. One team proposes 10 and the other proposes 11. If polling suggests that the 11 platform attracts less than a majority, then the team proposing 11 will change its platform to, say, 9, in the hope of attracting more support. This may lead the 10 team to propose 8. And so on, until new proposals fail to increase support. The point is that each team can only hope to win by appealing to the voter at the fiftieth percentile of ideal amounts of the collective good. Hence, the preferences of the median voter determine how much of the good we get through voting. So,

when does voting yield efficient results? When the median and mean voters have the same preferences. And this happens when the distribution of ideal amounts of the collective good is symmetric: for every person wanting one or two or three more dams than the median person wants, there is a person wanting the same one or two or three fewer dams than the median person wants. Symmetry fails when there is a disproportionate number of extremists on one side of an issue. The efficient result here still imposes a tyranny of the majority. Society gets what the median voter wants, and every other citizen gets something other than what he or she wants.

15. See Stigler (1971) for the classic statement of the argument.

16. See, for example, Savas (1982, 1987), Donahue (1989), or Kemp (1991).

17. See Shleifer and Vishny (1998) for characterization of government as a "grabbing hand." The World Bank's 1997 World Development Report provides an extensive discussion of corruption in developing countries.

3. Who Benefits Whom in Practice

1. Alex Berenson, "Blockbuster Drugs Are so Last Century," *New York Times,* July 3, 2005, sec. 3, p. 1.

2. Donald G. McNeil Jr., "Medicine Merchants: A Special Report; Drug Makers and Third World: Study in Neglect," *New York Times,* May 21, 2000, sec. 1, p. 1.

3. See "Table 2: Antisecretory Therapy for Peptic Ulcer Disease," www.clevelandclinicmeded.com (accessed 10/3/06); and "Acid Peptic Disorders," www.clevelandclinicmeded.com (accessed 10/3/06).

4. See "Erectile Dysfunction," kidney.niddk.nih.gov (accessed 7/20/05); "Medline Plus Medical Encyclopedia: Allergic Rhinitis," www.nlm.nih.gov (accessed 10/3/06); and Judy Foreman, "Orphan Diseases Leave Patients on Their Own," *Boston Globe,* June 28, 1999, p. C1.

5. See "Medline Plus Medical Encyclopedia: Sleeping Sickness," www.nlm.nih.gov (accessed 9/1/05).

6. See Coyne (2001).

7. See McNeil, "Medicine Merchants."

8. Ibid.

9. A Google search on "Eflornithine" on July 20, 2005, turns up ten sponsored sites offering facial hair removal products as well as nearly 50,000 others.

10. For example, Merck has donated 700 million tablets of Mectizan since

1987, effectively eradicating river blindness. See "Merck Donation Accelerates River Blindness Elimination in the Americas, May 19, 2004," www.cartercenter.org (accessed 9/22/05).

11. Including stations broadcasting from elsewhere but received in those cities, the numbers are 7 and 49, respectively. Stations in larger markets, with higher costs, require more listeners for viability.

12. See Waldfogel (2003) for discussion of this evidence.

13. Black people make up an average of 18.7 percent of the population in the 101 areas for which we have black listening data.

14. Blacks make up the majority of listeners to stations in five other formats: black/gospel, black/oldies, black/talk, gospel, and ethnic, which I term "black-targeted." Other formats attracting substantial amounts of black listening include contemporary hit radio/urban and jazz.

15. The urban/adult contemporary chart is posted at "Urban Adult Contemporary," www.radioandrecords.com (accessed 11/1/04).

16. The adult contemporary chart is posted at "Adult Contemporary," www.radioandrecords.com (accessed 11/1/04).

17. Philadelphia's black-targeted "urban adult contemporary" station WDAS-FM provides an illustrative example. See "On-Air Personalities," www.wdasfm.com (accessed 11/1/04).

18. Age and gender comparisons are based on 1993 listening data. See Waldfogel (1999) for a more detailed description of these data and comparisons of radio listening patterns by age and gender.

19. See Waldfogel (2003) for the data analyses underlying these statements.

20. See "Table 1. United States—Race and Hispanic Origin: 1780 to 1990," www.census.gov (accessed 10/3/06); and "The Hispanic Population: Census 2000 Brief," www.census.gov (accessed 10/3/06).

21. See Mark Fitzgerald, "Newspapers Rock en Español," *Editor and Publisher,* March 1, 2004.

22. See Gentzkow (2006).

23. See Fitzgerald, "Newspapers Rock."

24. Ibid.

25. Lance DeHaven-Smith, quoted in Dana Canedy, "Florida Has More Hispanics than Blacks, Census Shows," *New York Times,* March 28, 2001, sec. 1, p. 13.

26. Ibid.

27. This market share is calculated as tabloid circulation/(tabloid + broadsheet circulation).

28. A statistical analysis including other zip-code demographic characteris-

tics shows that the broadsheet newspaper earns a larger market share in zip codes with a higher fraction of residents who are white, non-Hispanic, college educated, high income, and younger than age sixty-five. Even after accounting for these other factors, the fraction of black residents in the zip code bears a strong positive relationship to tabloid market share. Summing up, even though these data show differences in newspaper preferences by race, there is no compelling evidence that blacks prefer these options because of race.

29. Empirical findings in this section are drawn from George and Waldfogel (2003).

4. Who Benefits Whom in the Neighborhood

1. The restaurant industry is also of some intrinsic interest owing to its size. A half million U.S. restaurants generate an annual revenue of $250 billion.

2. The analysis in this chapter is described in more detail in Waldfogel (2004).

3. I have data on the total number of restaurants—both chain and nonchain—and population at the zip code level, drawn from the 2002 Zip Code Business Patterns (ZBP) and the 2000 Census, respectively. The restaurants include all establishments in the Census's North American Industry Classification System (NAICS) code 722, Food Service and Drinking Places.

4. Note that this is the mean of radii, rather than the radius of an area the size of the mean area.

5. These data are drawn from "The QSR 50," www.qsrmagazine.com (accessed 9/13/2004). The twenty largest restaurant chains, in order, are McDonald's ($20.3 billion in 2002 revenue), Burger King ($8.7 billion), Wendy's ($7.1 billion), Subway ($5.2 billion), Taco Bell ($5.2 billion), Pizza Hut ($5.1 billion), KFC ($4.8 billion), Starbucks ($2.8 billion), Domino's Pizza ($2.9 billion), Dunkin' Donuts ($2.7 billion), Arby's ($2.7 billion), Sonic ($2.2 billion), Jack in the Box ($2.2 billion), Dairy Queen ($2.2 billion), Hardee's ($1.8 billion), Papa John's Pizza ($1.7 billion), Chick-fil-A ($1.4 billion), Popeye's Chicken and Biscuits ($1.3 billion), Little Caesars Pizza ($1.2 billion), and Carl's Jr. ($1.1 billion).

6. The Consumer Reports data are drawn from "Chain Restaurants: Best Meals, Best Deals," *Consumer Reports* (July 2003): 18–23.

7. Some part of the difference between black and white patronage rates is attributable to "constraints" such as restaurant availability and income levels rather than "preferences" per se. While we do not know the location of blacks with the sixty-six metro areas covered by Scarborough, we do know income, age, gender, and so on. Even after accounting for available characteristics—including metropolitan area, gender, and age—blacks are roughly 20 percentage points more likely (twice as likely at KFC and three times as likely at Popeye's) to patronize the chicken chains than are whites.

8. From "A History of Soul Food," www.foxhome.com (accessed 8/18/04). See also Kraft Foods' "African American Flavor Center," www.kraftfoods.com (accessed 8/18/04).

9. See "The Hispanic Population, Census 2000 Brief," www.census.gov (accessed 10/3/06).

10. Consumer Reports (2003).

11. See Waldfogel (2006).

12. It seems an overstatement to declare that persons without a sample chicken restaurant lack "access" to chicken, or even to sample chicken chains. After all, five-digit zip codes are small enough that a consumer certainly could travel to a nearby zip code, even if, on balance, consumers appear not to. We can get a sense of what our measure of access means by calculating the presence of groups of chains for four-digit zip codes that, you may recall, have an average radius of over six miles. And, indeed, just over half of four-digit zip codes have at least one sample chicken chain. But 70 percent of heavily black four-digit zip codes (those with populations over a third black) have at least one sample chicken chain. It is clearly more costly to travel farther, so the lack of a sample chicken chain within six miles provides a slightly stronger measure of privation than a similar lack within three miles.

13. See Black et al. (2002).

14. See Massey and Denton (1993).

15. See Tiebout (1958).

5. Preference Minorities as Citizens and Consumers

1. See "History of the Right to Vote in the U.S.," www.lwvabc.org (accessed 12/29/04).

2. Johnny Diaz, "Region to Get First Spanish Newscast Beginning in Spring at Studio in Needham," *Boston Globe*, February 6, 2003, p. A1.

3. Ibid.

4. Ibid.

5. Johnny Diaz, "Spanish Newscast Based in Needham to Debut Tuesday," *Boston Globe,* March 30, 2003, p. A1.

6. See Riker and Ordeshook (1968) for an argument that voting is puzzling behavior.

7. See Adam Segal, "Total 2004 Spanish-Language TV Ad Spending by Market and Campaign," February 2006, at advanced.jhu.edu (accessed 7/31/06).

8. The evidence in this chapter on Spanish-language local news and Hispanic voter turnout is drawn from Oberholzer-Gee and Waldfogel (2006).

9. Quotes drawn from "Univision and Telefutura Television Groups, Our Story," www.univision.net (accessed 12/30/04).

10. Telemundo was formed in 1986 by Saul Steinberg and Henry Silverman of Reliance Capital Group, L. P. See "Telemundo—Corporate Information," www.telemundo.com (accessed 12/30/04).

11. Most of the difference is attributable to the difference between the Hispanic and non-Hispanic age and education distributions. After accounting for education and age, the gap falls from fifteen to about five percentage points.

12. The evidence on black-targeted local media and black voter turnout is described in more detail in Oberholzer-Gee and Waldfogel (2005).

6. Market Enlargement and Consumer Liberation

1. See "Chronology of the Sears Catalog," www.searsarchives.com (accessed 9/29/05).

2. See Chapter 9 for more details about Wal-Mart's product selection, along with references.

3. Of course, this freedom is not complete, as the evidence of Part II emphasizes.

4. See "Volkswagen Beetle: Information from Answers.com," www.answers.com (accessed 10/3/06).

5. See "Technical Specifications of 1964 Pontiac Tempest" and "Technical Specifications of Chevrolet Corvair," www.carfolio.com (accessed 10/3/06).

6. See Bill Vlasic, "Getting Personal: One Size No Longer Fits All as Automakers Scramble to Design Models for Every Niche," *Detroit News,* January 9, 2005.

7. For the *Munsters* description, see "*Munsters:* Tvland.com," www.tvland.com (accessed 7/26/05).

8. See Julie Salamon, "The Road to Oprah," *New York Times,* February 18, 2001, sec. 7, p. 22.

9. Newton Minow, speech to the National Association of Broadcasters, Washington, D.C., May 9, 1961.

10. "By 2002, about 280 nationally-delivered cable networks were available, with that number growing steadily." See "History of Cable Television," www.ncta.com (accessed 12/22/04).

11. See "Packages: America's Everything Pack," www.dishnetwork.com (accessed 7/26/05).

12. All statistics are from the 2000 U.S. Census, "American Factfinder," factfinder.census.gov (accessed 1/6/05).

13. Ian Buruma, "Letter from Amsterdam," *New Yorker,* January 3, 2005, p. 26.

14. All of these channel descriptions are from "Comparison of Packages," www.directv.com (accessed 1/6/05).

15. See Joel Waldfogel, "Consumer Substitution among Media," Washington, D.C.: Federal Communications Commission, 2002 (available at www.fcc.gov/mb/mbpapers.html).

16. I visited the Sears store at King of Prussia Mall on September 24, 2005. Lands' End Men's vintage khaki pants were available in one color in waist sizes 32, 34, 36, 38, 40, and 42. Online, eight colors were available, in even- and odd-sized waistlines and with hems adjustable to quarter-inch increments.

17. See Robert W. Fairlie, "Race and the Digital Divide," *Contributions to Economic Analysis and Policy* 3 (2004): article 15; http://www.bepress.com/ bejeap/contributions/vol3/iss1/art15 (accessed 12/1/06).

18. This research is discussed in more detail in Sinai and Waldfogel (2004).

7. Fixed Costs, Product Quality, and Market Size

1. See "Zagat Survey: Find a Restaurant in/near Minnesota," www.zagat.com (accessed 6/29/05); and Jeremy Iggers, "Cuisine, Criticisms Both Changed with the Times," *Minneapolis Star Tribune,* November 4, 2004, p. T10.

2. This theme is explored extensively in the work of John Sutton and Avner Shaked. See Sutton (1991).

3. The paper, ink, and delivery required for the production and distribution of newspapers are exceptions to this claim. Still, I would argue that their contribution to the difference in quality across newspapers is small compared with the contribution of the reporters and editors.

4. See Berry and Waldfogel (2003).

8. Trade and the Tyranny of Alien Majorities

1. See "Seattle under Siege," www.urban75.com (accessed 6/1/05).

2. See Stiglitz (2002), which explains many of the objections to globalization.

3. See Tyler Cowen, "French Kiss-Off: How Protectionism Has Hurt French Films," *Reason*, 1998 (accessed at http://reason.com/9807/fe.cowen.shtml, 9/29/05).

4. See Pindyck and Rubinfeld (2001), p. 310.

5. See Catherine Lalumière, French member of the European parliament, "The Battle of 'Cultural Diversity,'" www.france.diplomatie.fr (accessed 6/1/05).

6. See chapter 5 of Waterman (2005).

7. See Lynn Hirschberg, "What Is an American Movie Now?" *New York Times*, November 14, 2004, sec. 6 (*Sunday Magazine*), p. 89.

8. Ibid.

9. Ibid.

10. Ibid.

11. All quotations in this paragraph are from ibid.

12. See "Supplementary Survey 2001 Profile, Population and Housing Profile: New Haven—Meriden, CT PMSA," www.census.gov (accessed 10/3/06).

13. See "Supplementary Survey 2001 Profile, Population and Housing Profile: The United States," www.census.gov (accessed 10/3/06).

14. See "*New Haven Register* Reader Profile, Feb. 2004–Jan. 2005," abcas3.accessabc.com (accessed 10/3/06).

15. This evidence is drawn from George and Waldfogel (2006).

9. Salvation through New Technologies

1. See Solow (1957).

2. See "The Showroom of Automotive History: Model T Specifications," www.hfmgv.org (accessed 10/3/06).

3. See "Time 100: Henry Ford," www.time.com (accessed 10/3/06).

4. See www.sirius.com and www.xmradio.com for information about the two satellite radio offerings available in the United States (accessed 9/20/05).

5. See "The Boeing Next-Generation 737–700 Convertible," www.boeing.com (accessed 10/3/06).

6. Micheline Maynard, "In Airline Shift, More Nonstop Flights Make Schedule," *New York Times,* May 4, 2005, p. A1.

7. James Fallows, "Fly Me to the Moon? No, But the Next Best Thing," *New York Times,* July 10, 2005, sec. 3, p. 3.

8. Ibid.

9. All quotes in this subsection are from Alex Berenson, "Blockbuster Drugs Are so Last Century," *New York Times,* July 3, 2005, sec. 3, p. 1.

10. See "Chronology of the Sears Catalog," www.searsarchives.com (accessed 9/20/05).

11. See p. 7 of "Best Buy Fiscal 2004 Annual Report," www.bby communications.com (accessed 7/31/06).

12. Some facts from "Wal-Mart," en.wikipedia.org (accessed 9/20/05).

13. See "Wal-Mart Names New Retailing Concept: The Wal-Mart Neighborhood Market, July 10, 1998," www.walmartstores.com (accessed 9/20/05).

14. Ibid.

15. The friction between economists and scientists is evident in discussions about how much oil is left to be extracted. See Joseph Nocera, "On Oil Supply, Opinions Aren't Scarce," *New York Times,* September 10, 2005, sec. 3, p. 1.

10. Government Subsidies and Insufficient Demand

1. Ralph Blumenthal, "In the Age of the Wireless Phone, a Louisiana Town Awaits the Real Thing," *New York Times,* December 12, 2004, sec. 1, p. 37.

2. Ibid.

3. Jake Thompson, "Subsidies Remain Airborne," *Omaha World Herald,* July 27, 2005, p. B11.

4. See *Commercial Aviation: Factors Affecting Efforts to Improve Air Service at Small Community Airports* (Washington, D.C.: General Accounting Office, January 2003), p. 12.

5. The flight data are for flights on October 26, 2005, and are from the "OAG Airline and Airport Guide," www.oag.com (accessed 10/26/05 and 12/1/06).

6. Both quotes in this paragraph are from U.S. Department of Transportation, Office of Aviation Analysis, "What Essential Air Service?" May 1, 1998, at ostpxweb.dot.gov (accessed 10/3/06).

7. See "U.S. Department of Transportation Budget," www.whitehouse.gov (accessed 10/3/06).

8. See "Essential Air Service Program," ostpxweb.dot.gov (accessed 10/3/06).

9. See "Small Community Air Service Development Program," ostpxweb.dot.gov (accessed 10/3/06).

10. "The Department's mandate is to provide the EAS communities with access to the national air transportation system. As a general matter, this is accomplished by subsidizing two to four round trips a day—with three being the norm—with 19-seat aircraft to a major hub airport." See "Essential Air Service Program," ostpxweb.dot.gov (accessed 10/3/06).

11. See "Other Press Releases," www.greatlakesav.com (accessed 6/9/05).

12. See "Budget of the United States Government, FY 2006, Table S-1. Budget Totals," www.whitehouse.gov (accessed 10/3/06).

13. See "National Plan of Integrated Airport Systems," www.faa.gov (accessed 10/3/06).

14. See "Airport Improvement Program," www.federalgrantswire.com (accessed 10/3/06).

15. See "Congressional Rural Caucus," www.house.gov/johnpeterson/rural caucus (accessed 06/28/05); and "Congressional Rural Caucus Leadership and Member List," www.house.gov (accessed 7/28/05).

16. Thompson, "Subsidies Remain Airborne."

17. David C. Beeder, "House Panel OKs Rural Air Subsidy Funds," *Omaha World Herald,* June 23, 1995, p. 8. Barrett's sentiments sound a little odd when juxtaposed with comments by Republican former FCC head Michael K. Powell. When asked about the "digital divide," a term used to describe depressed minority access to the Internet, Powell answered, "I think there's a Mercedes divide. I'd like to have one; I can't afford one." Quoted in Stephen Labaton, "New F.C.C. Chief Would Curb Agency Reach," *New York Times,* February 7, 2001, sec. 3, p. 1.

18. See Berry and Waldfogel (1999b).

19. See 2003 revenue data at "Who Pays for Public Broadcasting," www.cpb.org (accessed 9/13/05).
20. See "Radio Wraps Up 2003 with Ad Sales Slightly Ahead of Last Year, New York, New York—February 2, 2004," www.rab.com (accessed 9/13/05).
21. See "CPB: Mission Statement," www.cpb.org (accessed 10/3/06).
22. Budget figures are from "2004 Budget," www.cpb.org (accessed 10/3/06).
23. The evidence in this section draws on Berry and Waldfogel (1999b).
24. See Siegelman and Waldfogel (2001).
25. See Universal Service Administrative Company, *Annual Report* 2003, p. 12, at www.universalservice.org (accessed 8/1/06).
26. Ibid., p. 27.
27. Rural Utilities Service, *Annual Report 2003* (Washington, D.C.: U.S. Department of Agriculture, 2003), p. 1.
28. Ibid., pp. 7–9.
29. Ibid.

11. Books and Liquor: Two Case Studies

1. UPS rates were obtained from "UPS Calculate Time and Cost," wwwapps.ups.com (accessed 7/6/05).
2. U.S. Postal Service rates were obtained from "Postal Rate Calculator," postcalc.usps.gov (accessed 7/6/05).
3. From "Philadelphia Neighborhood Profile, Location: Philadelphia 19132," http://realestate.yahoo.com (accessed 10/3/06).
4. See, for example, Savas (1982, 1987); Donahue (1989); or Kemp (1991). Other scholars focus on corruption as an endemic feature of government allocation; see Shleifer and Vishny (1998).
5. See Bresnahan and Reiss (1990, 1991).
6. From a speech by Amy Dougherty, executive director of the Friends of the Free Library of Philadelphia, "State Legislative Issues," www.libraryfriends.info (accessed 9/7/05).
7. For a discussion of the history of private libraries in the United States, see Richard Roehl and Hal R. Varian, "Circulating Libraries and Video Rental Stores," *First Monday* 2001 (peer-reviewed journal on the Internet; this article is available at ttp://www.firstmonday.org/issues/issue6_5/roehl/#r0).

8. See "The Library Company," www.ushistory.org (accessed 9/25/06).

9. See "A Brief History and Description," www.bpl.org (Boston Public Library website, accessed 5/18/05).

10. See George S. Bobinski, "History of the Carnegie Libraries," www.carnegie-libraries.org (accessed 5/18/05).

11. See "1997 Economic Census: Retail Trade," www.census.gov (accessed 5/18/05). Of the $17 billion figure for the publishing industry, $4.2 billion was for trade books, while roughly $8 billion was for professional and educational books. If municipal libraries' collections consist mainly of trade books, then library expenditures appear to make up a sizable share of national expenditure on trade books (roughly a sixth).

12. See "Store Locator," www.bordersstores.com, and "Store Locator," storelocator.barnesandnoble.com (both accessed 5/12/05).

13. State Representative Mark Buesgens, "News Release: Buesgens Introduces Legislation to End Government Monopolies of Alcohol Sales," May 26, 2005. At www.house.leg.state.mn.us (accessed 7/15/05).

14. T. W. Budig, "Capitol Notebook: State Auditor Awada Expresses Concern over Liquor Store Monies," *ECM Capitol Reporter,* June 4, 2003. At www.hometownsource.com (accessed 7/15/05).

15. A second point is that people may underestimate the benefit of their exposure to books. Not only does the reader benefit, through his entertainment and edification; others also benefit as the reader becomes better equipped to succeed in school and in society. "Libraries are in the business of prevention—as a provider of education and job readiness—libraries help prevent joblessness that often leads to crime, drug use, and unstable neighborhoods." See "State Legislative Issues," www.libraryfriends.info (accessed 8/2/06). In short, library use creates what economists term a "positive externality." This is one of the standard reasons why markets are believed to fail. I have not availed myself of this argument in the book because my goal is to show some features of how markets function in situations where they are broadly believed to work.

Conclusion

1. See, for example, Cutler and Glaeser (1997), Cutler, Glaeser, and Vigdor (1999), or Massey and Denton (1993).

2. See Breyer (1982).

3. See U.S. Department of Justice and the Federal Trade Commission, *Horizontal Merger Guidelines,* issued April 2, 1992; revised April 8, 1997 (available at www.usdoj.gov/atr/public/guidelines/horiz_book/hmg1.htm; accessed 10/3/06).

4. This discussion draws on Berry and Waldfogel (2001).

5. See George (2001).

6. These arguments—and their variants—are explored in Wolf (1988).

7. These arguments are discussed in Shleifer and Vishny (1998).

8. "President Honors Milton Friedman for Lifetime Achievement, Remarks by President in Tribute to Milton Friedman, May 9, 2002," www.whitehouse.gov (accessed 12/1/06).

References

Akerlof, George A. 1970. "The Market for 'Lemons': Quality Uncertainty and the Market Mechanism." *Quarterly Journal of Economics* 84: 488–500.

Arbitron Company. 1994. *Radio Metro Market Guide, 1993–1994.* New York: Arbitron Company.

———. 1997. *Radio USA.* New York: Arbitron Company.

Ayres, Ian. 2002. *Pervasive Prejudice? Non-Traditional Evidence of Race and Gender Discrimination.* Chicago: University of Chicago Press.

Becker, Gary S. 1971. *The Economics of Discrimination,* 2d ed. Chicago: University of Chicago Press.

Berry, Steven T., and Joel Waldfogel. 1999a. "Free Entry and Social Inefficiency in Radio Broadcasting." *RAND Journal of Economics* 30: 397–420.

———. 1999b. "Public Radio in the United States: Does It Correct Market Failure or Cannibalize Commercial Stations?" *Journal of Public Economics* 71: 189–211.

———. 2001. "Mergers and Product Variety: Evidence from Radio Broadcasting." *Quarterly Journal of Economics* 116: 1009–1025.

———. 2003. "Product Quality and Market Size." Working paper 9675, National Bureau of Economic Research (NBER), Cambridge.

Black, Dan, et al. 2002. "Why Do Gay Men Live in San Francisco?" *Journal of Urban Economics* 51: 54–76.

Bresnahan, Timothy F., and Peter C. Reiss. 1990. "Entry in Monopoly Markets." *Review of Economic Studies* 57: 531–553.

———. 1991. "Entry and Competition in Concentrated Markets." *Journal of Political Economy* 99: 977–1009.

Breyer, Stephen. 1982. *Regulation and Its Reform*. Cambridge: Harvard University Press.

Burrelle's Information Services. 2000. *Burrelle's Media Directory*. Livingston, N.J.: Burrelle's Information Services.

Coase, Ronald A. 1960. "The Problem of Social Cost." *Journal of Law and Economics* 3: 1–44.

Consumer Reports. 2003. "Best Meals, Best Deals." *Consumer Reports* (July): 18–23.

Coyne, Philip E. 2001. "The Eflornithine Story." *Journal of American Academic Dermatology* 45: 784–786.

Cutler, David M., and Edward L. Glaeser. 1997. "Are Ghettos Good or Bad?" *Quarterly Journal of Economics* 112: 827–872.

Cutler, David M., Edward L. Glaeser, and Jacob L. Vigdor. 1999. "The Rise and Decline of the American Ghetto." *Journal of Political Economy* 107: 455–506.

d'Aspremont, Claude, Jean Jaskold-Gabszewicz, and Jacques-François Thisse. 1979. "On Hotelling's 'Stability in Competition.'" *Econometrica* 47: 1145–1150.

Dixit, Avinash K., and Joseph E. Stiglitz. 1997. "Monopolistic Competition and Optimum Product Diversity." *American Economic Review* 67: 297–308.

Donahue, John D. 1989. *The Privatization Decision: Public Ends, Private Means*. New York: Basic Books.

Duncan, James H. 1993. *Duncan's American Radio, Spring 1993*. Indianapolis: Duncan's American Radio.

———. 1994. *Duncan's Radio Market Guide*. Indianapolis: Duncan's American Radio.

———. 1997. *Duncan's American Radio, Spring 1997*. Indianapolis: Duncan's American Radio.

Economides, Nicholas. 1989. "Quality Variations and Maximal Variety Differentiation." *Regional Science and Urban Economics* 19: 21–29.

———. 1993. "Hotelling's 'Main Street' with More than Two Competitors." *Journal of Regional Science* 33: 303–319.

Fehr, Ernst, and Klaus M. Schmidt. 1999. "A Theory of Fairness, Competition, and Cooperation." *Quarterly Journal of Economics* 114: 817–868.

Friedman, Milton. 1962. *Capitalism and Freedom*. Chicago: University of Chicago Press.

Gentzkow, Matthew. 2006. "Television and Voter Turnout." *Quarterly Journal of Economics* 121: 931–972.

George, Lisa. 2001. "What's Fit to Print: The Effect of Ownership Concentration on Product Variety in Daily Newspaper Markets." Unpublished paper, Hunter College.

George, Lisa, and Joel Waldfogel. 2003. "Who Affects Whom in Daily Newspaper Markets?" *Journal of Political Economy* 111: 765–784.

———. 2006. "The *New York Times* and the Market for Local Newspapers." *American Economic Review* 96: 435–447.

Glaeser, Edward L., Jed Kolko, and Albert Saiz. 2001. "Consumer City," *Journal of Economic Geography* 1: 27–50.

Guth, Werner, Rolf Schmittberger, and Bernd Schwarze. 1982. "An Experimental Analysis of Ultimatum Bargaining." *Journal of Economic Behavior and Organization* 3: 367–388.

Heal, Geoffrey. 1980. "Spatial Structure in Retail Trade: A Study in Product Differentiation." *Bell Journal of Economics* 11: 565–583.

Hotelling, Harold. 1929. "Stability in Competition." *Economic Journal* 39: 41–57.

Kemp, Roger L., ed. 1991. *Privatization: The Provision of Public Services by the Private Sector.* Jefferson, N.C.: McFarland & Co.

Mankiw, N. Gregory, and Michael D. Whinston. 1986. "Free Entry and Social Inefficiency." *RAND Journal of Economics* 17: 48–58.

Massey, Douglas, and Nancy Denton. 1993. *American Apartheid: Segregation and the Making of the Underclass.* Cambridge: Harvard University Press.

Mazzeo, Michael J. 2002. "Product Choice and Oligopoly Market Structure." *RAND Journal of Economics* 33: 1–22.

Mill, John Stuart. 1978. *On Liberty.* Indianapolis: Hacket.

Oberholzer-Gee, Felix, and Joel Waldfogel. 2005. "Strength in Numbers: Group Size and Political Mobilization." *Journal of Law and Economics* 48: 75–91.

———. 2006. "Does Local News *en Español* Raise Hispanic Voter Turnout?" Working paper 12317, National Bureau of Economic Research (NBER), Cambridge.

Oberholzer-Gee, Felix, Joel Waldfogel, and Matthew White. 2003. "Social Learning and Coordination in High-Stakes Games: Evidence from Friend or Foe," Working paper 9805, National Bureau of Economic Research (NBER), Cambridge.

Pindyck, Robert S., and Daniel L. Rubinfeld. 2001. *Microeconomics,* 5th ed. Upper Saddle River, N.J.: Prentice Hall.

Rabin, M. 1993. "Incorporating Fairness into Game Theory and Economics." *American Economic Review* 83: 1281–1302.

Riker, William H., and Peter C. Ordeshook. 1968. "A Theory of the Calculus of Voting." *American Political Science Review* 62: 25–42.

Savas, E. S. 1982. *Privatizing the Public Sector: How to Shrink Government.* Chatham, N.J.: Chatham House.

———. 1987. *Privatization: The Key to Better Government.* Chatham, N.J.: Chatham House.

Shleifer, Andre, and Robert Vishny. 1998. *The Grabbing Hand.* Cambridge: Harvard University Press.

Siegelman, Peter, and Joel Waldfogel. 2001. "Race and Radio: Preference Externalities, Minority Ownership, and the Provision of Programming to Minorities." In *Advances in Applied Microeconomics,* vol. 10, ed. Michael R. Baye and Jon P. Nelson, pp. 73–108. Greenwich, Conn.: JAI Press.

Sinai, Todd M., and Joel Waldfogel. 2004. "Geography and the Internet: Is the Internet a Substitute or a Complement for Cities?" *Journal of Urban Economics* 56: 1–24.

Solow, Robert M. 1957. "Technical Change and the Aggregate Production Function." *Review of Economics and Statistics* 39: 312–320.

Spence, Michael. 1976a. "Product Selection, Fixed Costs, and Monopolistic Competition." *Review of Economic Studies* 43: 217–235.

———. 1976b. "Product Differentiation and Welfare." *American Economic Review* 66: 407–414.

Stigler, George J. 1971. "The Theory of Economic Regulation." *Bell Journal of Economics* 2: 3–21.

Stiglitz, Joseph E. 1996. *Whither Socialism?* Cambridge: MIT Press.

———. 2002. *Globalization and Its Discontents.* New York: W. W. Norton.

Sutton, John. 1991. *Sunk Costs and Market Structure.* Cambridge: MIT Press.

Tiebout, Charles. 1958. "A Pure Theory of Local Expenditures." *Journal of Political Economy* 114: 416–424.

Waldfogel, Joel. 1999. "Preference Externalities: An Empirical Study of Who Benefits Whom in Differentiated Product Markets." Working paper 7391, National Bureau of Economic Research (NBER), Cambridge.

———. 2003. "Preference Externalities: An Empirical Study of Who Benefits Whom in Differentiated Product Markets." *RAND Journal of Economics* 34: 557–568.

———. 2004. "Who Benefits Whom in Local Television Markets?" *Brookings-Wharton Papers on Urban Affairs* 5: 257–284.

———. 2006. "The Median Voter and the Median Consumer." Working paper 11972, National Bureau of Economic Research (NBER), Cambridge.

Waterman, David. 2005. *Hollywood's Road to Riches.* Cambridge: Harvard University Press.

Wolf, Charles, Jr. 1988. *Markets or Governments: Choosing between Imperfect Alternatives.* Cambridge: MIT Press.

World Bank. 1997. *World Development Report: The State in a Changing World.* New York: Oxford University Press.

Credits

In writing this book, I drew on a number of my previously published technical papers, some of them coauthored. In every case the papers were completely rewritten and augmented with additional ideas, so they bear little resemblance to the chapters here. I list them below, however, for readers who may be interested in a technical presentation of some of the content of this book.

Joel Waldfogel, "Preference Externalities: An Empirical Study of Who Benefits Whom in Differentiated Product Markets," Working Paper 7391, National Bureau of Economic Research, 1999. © 1999 by Joel Waldfogel.

Peter Siegelman and Joel Waldfogel, "Race and Radio: Preference Externalities, Minority Ownership, and the Provision of Programming to Minorities," *Advances in Applied Microeconomics* 10 (2001): 73–107. © 2001 by Elsevier Science Ltd. All rights of reproduction in any form reserved.

Joel Waldfogel, "Preference Externalities: An Empirical Study of Who Benefits Whom in Differentiated-Product Markets," *RAND Journal of Economics* 34, no. 3 (Autumn 2003): 557–568. © 2003, RAND.

Steven Berry and Joel Waldfogel. "Product Quality and Market Size" Working Paper 9675, National Bureau of Economic Research. © 2003 by Steven Berry and Joel Waldfogel.

Lisa George and Joel Waldfogel, "Who Affects Whom in Daily Newspaper Markets?" *Journal of Political Economy* 111, no. 41 (2003). © 2003 by The University of Chicago. All rights reserved.

Frank R. Lichtenberg and Joel Waldfogel, "Does Misery Love Company? Evidence from Pharmaceutical Markets before and after the Orphan

Index